My First Exorcism

My First Exorcism

What the Devil Taught a Lutheran Pastor
about Counter-cultural Spirituality

by
REV. DR. HAROLD RISTAU

Foreword by
REV. DR. JOHN W. KLEINIG

RESOURCE *Publications* • Eugene, Oregon

MY FIRST EXORCISM
What the Devil Taught a Lutheran Pastor about Counter-cultural Spirituality

Copyright © 2016 Harold Ristau. All rights reserved. Except for brief quotations in critical publications or reviews, no part of this book may be reproduced in any manner without prior written permission from the publisher. Write: Permissions, Wipf and Stock Publishers, 199 W. 8th Ave., Suite 3, Eugene, OR 97401.

Resource Publications
An Imprint of Wipf and Stock Publishers
199 W. 8th Ave., Suite 3
Eugene, OR 97401

www.wipfandstock.com

PAPERBACK ISBN 13: 978-1-4982-2571-7
HARDCOVER ISBN 13: 978-1-4982-2573-1

Manufactured in the U.S.A.   04/13/2016

Scripture quotations are from The Holy Bible, English Standard Version* (ESV*), copyright © 2001 by Crossway, a publishing ministry of Good News Publishers. Used by permission. All rights reserved.

Dedicated to all the faithful soldiers
who have shaken hands with the devil
and lived to tell their stories.

If you want to change the world, pick up your pen and write.
—Martin Luther

I thank you, my heavenly Father, through Jesus Christ, Your dear Son, that You have kept me this night from all harm and danger; and I pray that You would keep me this day also from sin and every evil, that all my doings and life may please You. For into Your hands I commend myself, my body and soul, and all things. Let Your holy angel be with me, that the evil foe may have no power over me. Amen.

—Martin Luther's Morning Prayer

Contents

Foreword by Rev. Dr. John W. Kleinig | ix
Abbreviations | xiii

Prologue: A Hitchhiker's Guide to the Demonic | 1
A Midsummer's Nightmare | 12
The Art of Exorcising | 28
Who's Afraid of the Steppenwolf? | 44
The Lion, the Witch and the Lord's Supper | 80
The World According to *der Zeitgeist* | 92
The Purpose Driven Lie | 106
Le petit prince des ténèbres | 132
Why I am not *not* a Christian | 154
Epilogue: The Death of a Sales Pitch | 159

Bibliography | 165

Foreword

In his Preface to *The Screwtape Letters* in 1941, C. S. Lewis makes this shrewd observation:

> There are two equal and opposite errors into which our race can fall about the devils. One is to disbelieve their existence. The other is to believe, and to feel an excessive and unhealthy interest in them. They themselves are equally pleased by both errors and hail a materialist and a magician with the same delight.

I would add another pair. It is just as foolish for pastors to presume expertise in diabolical activity as to ignore it. One measure of an effective pastor is his ability to minister to people who are under spiritual attack and to learn from that experience. It makes for a better theologian as well.

A calm discussion on demon possession, like any serious theological reflection on it, is, of course, deeply embarrassing even in Christian circles in those countries shaped by the ideology of the Enlightenment. The worldview of the West erects an iron curtain between the natural, material world and the supernatural, spiritual over-world. It also completely discounts the existence of a supernatural, spiritual underworld. Thus both demons and the devil are, theoretically, expunged from the cosmos by definition. If only it were that easy! The possibility of their existence is ruled out, except, perhaps, as the phantasies of an unstable imagination. Yet, for all that, the demons refuse to be excluded. They still haunt us, even though we often have no idea as to what to do with them, let alone how to think of them.

In contrast to our society's denial of the demonic realm, most other cultures take the existence and activity of demons for granted. Thus the exorcism of demons is vital to the mission of the churches in non-Western countries. There evangelism involves the ministry of deliverance, for

Foreword

wherever the gospel is proclaimed in a pagan environment the demons emerge from hiding. They are required to be dealt with, spiritually. That too is increasingly the case in North America, Europe, and Australia, in the present aftermath of apostasy from Christ as the walls that have kept the demons at bay come down. Something is changing at the deepest levels of popular culture as the spiritual world is once again rediscovered by our compatriots in many different ways. This rediscovery has, in turn, produced a deep and yet somewhat indiscriminate interest in spirituality as they try to make sense of what they experience. It is not entirely clear why and how this has occurred. But it is, I believe, likely to accelerate.

This change of perception first struck me in my first years as a young pastor from 1969–1972, during a tumultuous time of social, cultural and religious upheaval that swept across the Western world. As a result of sexual experimentation, the use of hallucinogenic drugs, and the counter-culture that celebrated emotional liberation through them, young people experienced for themselves, emotionally and psychologically, imaginatively and cognitively, the wonderful and yet terrible realities of spiritual goodness and spiritual wickedness. As a result, there arose a call for teaching on spirituality and the need for deliverance from demonic darkness in all its ugly manifestations. I still remember, vividly, the first time an evil presence looked straight at me with malice and mockery through the eyes of a teenage girl and addressed me with an alien voice quite unlike her own. By sheer necessity I, like Harold Ristau, had to engage in the ministry of deliverance, something that I had not been trained to do. Both then and in later instances I was guided by what I knew from the ministry of Jesus in the Gospels and what I learned gradually from painful experience.

As I welcome this lively study by Harold Ristau on his first exorcism, I am grateful for his reflections on it, and for sharing all that he has learned from it. As a pastor and theologian I resonate with much of what he says. He speaks from within his tradition as an orthodox Lutheran pastor at a time when his church is rediscovering its own heritage of teaching on spiritual warfare. While his approach is popular and useful for any mature Christian, this book is addressed, mainly, to other pastors. It is not a handbook on exorcism or a pastoral treatise on the ministry of deliverance. It is, instead, an extended pastoral case study, based on and inspired by his first experience of an exorcism. It combines his description of that encounter with a Biblical and theological reflection on it, as well as the implications for his own theological and spiritual self-understanding. Thus, his intent is not to prescribe any particular method of exorcism, but to show how the ministry of deliverance is to be undertaken as part of the whole counsel of God, the whole of Christian doctrine, and the whole enactment of God's Word in the Divine Service.

Ristau is to be commended for his sober, pragmatic approach to an issue that is all too often treated sensationally. Contrary to popular misconceptions of demonization as a single, uniform state of oppression, there is a spectrum of demonic activity that ranges from accusation and condemnation to what is often described as demon possession. And each of these attacks needs to be dealt with differently. Since the devil is the master of chaos and confusion, the father of lies, it is unhelpful to look for order where it does not exist. Thus the pastor does well to deal with what is presented as it occurs, without undue reliance on any set pattern or a stock ritual procedure, in providing Christ's help for people under demonic assault. Every case is different. Accordingly, treatment is usually part of a process rather than a single dramatic event, a process in which the causes for attack are dealt with, new defenses are erected, and the soul is gradually healed.

Ristau is also to be commended for his consistent emphasis on the three basic, interrelated resources that are available to pastors for ministry to people who are under demonic or spiritual attack. First, exorcism is not an exercise in personal spiritual expertise or power; it is always the exercise of Christ's authority in the Office of the Ministry and of faith in Him. Thus the Office of the ordained ministry provides all that is needed for him to deal with the master of insubordination and his insubordinate cronies. By himself the pastor has no authority or power to silence the evil hosts and put them back to where they belong. He depends entirely on the authority of Jesus Christ and the power of His Holy Spirit.

Second, since exorcism depends on Christ's victory over the devil and all the powers of darkness, the pastor's basic weapon, his sword, is the Spirit-filled Word of God. God's Word alone has the power to penetrate the dark corners of the human heart and to drive the devil from the stronghold of the guilty conscience. When God's Word is spoken out aloud and addressed to the conscience of the hearer, the demons are unsettled, disempowered and put to flight. Of all God's words the most powerful is the most holy name of Jesus. Oftentimes, the reaction to that name exposes the spiritual state of the hearer. The proclamation and confession of Jesus as Lord brings deliverance.

Foreword

Third, since pastors, like the twelve apostles, are commissioned to drive out demons in the name of Jesus (Matt 10:1; Mark 6:7; Luke 9:1), they rely entirely on Christ's help in the ministry of deliverance by praying to the Father in His name. They ask for protection and guidance from the Triune God, best achieved by praying the Lord's Prayer. Therefore the ministry of deliverance is the faithful ministry of intercession which relies on God's Word to know what to pray for, and how. In moments of uncertainty and doubt, the pastor resorts to prayer for the troubled soul and himself as Christ's representative. By praying he, as it were, steps aside, so that the interaction between him and the harried soul becomes an encounter between Jesus and the devil, the Holy Spirit and the unclean spirit.

The anecdotal and reflective character of this book does not claim to provide its readers with the final word on demon possession and exorcism. It is, instead, a tentative exploration of the issue that aims to stimulate reflection and encourage action. More than anything else it sets out to give pastors confidence in helping people who are under demonic attack or disabled by the devil. By telling his story and sharing his personal reflections on its significance, Ristau encourages all pastors and faithful Christians to be vigilant against the devil in all his many guises and to resist him by their faith in Jesus (1 Pet 5:8–9).

Rev. Dr. John W. Kleinig

Abbreviations

AE   Luther's Works (American Edition). 55 vols. ed. Jaroslav Pelikan and Helmut T. Lehmann. Philadelphia: Muehlenberg and Fortress, and St. Louis: CPH, 1955–86.

LSB   Lutheran Service Book. Prepared by The Commission on Worship of The Lutheran Church—Missouri Synod. Saint Louis: CPH, 2006.

TLH   The Lutheran Hymnal. The Evangelical Lutheran Synodical Conference of North America. Saint Louis: CPH, 1941.

Prologue
A Hitchhiker's Guide to the Demonic

> Be sober-minded; be watchful. Your adversary the devil prowls around like a roaring lion, seeking someone to devour. (1 Pet 5:8)

Most people have seen the movie *The Exorcist*. If you haven't, I wouldn't recommend it. Nevertheless, it could be worse. The internet has opened wide a new horizon of occultist subject matter easily available for viewing, yet offering very few tools in determining the validity of the implied claims. Mildly amusing, *The Exorcist* is apparently "based on actual events." Hollywood is not accustomed to the academic practice of footnoting in substantiating its declarations. Viewers are just expected to believe. As a Christian, I find it inconceivable that the faithful priest was not successful in the end—especially after the sequel! As to the young girl's bleached white face, stained yellow teeth, bloodshot eyes and crusty cracked skin, I still have my doubts. In my limited encounters with demoniacs, I have yet to witness any of those symptoms. At the same time, the more I investigate the ancient texts and cases on record, the more questions I have. In general, the devil chooses to appear as an "angel of light" (2 Cor 11:14), while his collection of zombie costumes accumulates dust in the closet of his underworld apartment. His subtle tactics infiltrate the way we view the world and derive meaning from our experiences. Obviously, if the evil foe appeared in all of his natural ugliness, he would attract us less. A mere peek at his actual wardrobe may turn agnostics into Christians. As it stands, the majority of people have draped themselves with the subtleties of this dark prince's religions, philosophies, lifestyles and doctrines. No, the devil prefers sheep's clothing.

With the help of the evil one, the media and inferred religion of the surrounding culture perpetrate an anti-Christian spirituality. They discredit the vital value of tradition and wholesome religious customs by an implicit mockery of the wisdom of past generations and an insidious patronization of the elderly. They celebrate the "naturalism" of witchcraft as an off-shoot of the Green movement. They boast that the self-fulfilment and empowering abilities of Wicca are harmonious with the goals and values of our postmodern era. Yet Christians are not exempt from these temptations. Sadly, they show little resistance. For example, most consider horror movies harmless, as long as they teach a life lesson coherent with an agreeable moral value—and when they are not entirely fictional, they should end on a happy note. Depictions of violence are scarcely grounds to blush. Ungallant speech escapes unnoticed, exciting little suspicion in an already numbed brain. Sex scenes are a cinematographic red herring and thus rationalized as collateral damage to an edifying plot. Few scorn their shame, lulled by their disseminating poison. Most bravely indulge this eye candy with no regret or apprehension. Scenes of a sensual nature between married couples trick us into believing that the R-Rated film is somehow less pornographic. Voyeurism is justified as "educational" when the story is inspired by factual events.

Like many kids, as a youngster, I was intrigued by scary movies. I guess that most young boys like a thrill, while preadolescent imagination tries to imitate those curious things seen on TV. My mischievous friends and I would occasionally play with *Ouija*. Sometimes strange things would happen. Although there was a lot of goofing around, I am convinced that at least on one occasion, a non-human entity attempted to convey a message. We all ran out of the room screaming. Moments later, the fright was followed by giggles, laughing, and other forms of playful accusations and silliness. Despite harmless intentions, I am persuaded that we had accessed a portal to the demonic realm. The monsters in my closet seemed a lot more real after that. The basement felt darker; the breathing in the bedroom closet, heavier. All kids have bad dreams. But my nightmares came with a vengeance, consuming most of the week's sleeps. They were accompanied by hallucinations and inexplicable fainting spells recurring over the course of years. Praise God for my guardian angel! Overreaction? Oversensitivity? Maybe. Thankfully, the intensity of these dreadful dreams receded after I joined a Bible study group as a teenager. Eventually they dissipated entirely.

Prologue

But many of the images and themes remained imbedded in my Freudian ego. They are probably still there—I still like scary movies.

As Christians, we are emancipated from the power and condemnation of the Law. Simply put, no one has the right to insist that we must abide by a new collection of Talmudic principles, even if some of them make a lot of sense. God's people reside under the umbrella of grace. Sinners no longer pummelled by the hailstorm of legalistic obligations are "free." But are we at liberty to watch the enemies of Christ and His Gospel applaud their dark conduct, making jest of our persecuted Lord, even if it does not jeopardize our status as His servants? Would a married man choose to tolerate some jealous scoundrel habitually slandering his wife, even if it would never result in a divorce? The Apostle encourages believers to dwell on topics that are honourable, pure and lovely (Phil 4:8) as the overall healthier choice. Questionable decisions may not change our position before the throne of grace in heaven, but may certainly impact our level of personal misery until we get there. Besides, they lack class.

The memoirs recorded and commentaries penned in this book are intended to educate and persuade the reader in matters pertaining to the demonic realm. Perhaps this humble and tiny contribution will serve as one of many other sources of corporate memory for the Church. The Word of God challenges us "not to be outwitted by Satan" by being "ignorant of his designs" (2 Cor 2:11). Flung headlong from the heights of heaven, the devil prowls around like a vicious lion "going to and fro on the earth, and from walking up and down on it" (Job 2:2). My hope is that the Christian reader will spiritually profit through a deeper understanding of the devil's machinations, being better equipped with the full armour of God in the spiritual battles against the dark principalities in which we daily engage.

The military would liken such a project to an "After Action Report" with the purpose of learning lessons from the successes and errors of others. However, normally such debriefings are compiled immediately after a critical incident occurs. My stories, however, are not recent. Some of them are nearly a quarter-century old. Why bring them up now? Frankly, after an early episode with exorcism, I had convinced myself that no right-minded person would hear me without a suspension of disbelief. We are all biased. After being rewarded with a burst of laughter the first time around, I decided that I would only share my experiences amongst believers with whom I was guaranteed to escape judgment as gullible or jeered at as superstitious. Today, I care less.

Most educated people believe that what we call "demon possession" is simply a dubious expression of mental illness, satisfactorily treated by pharmaceuticals. After all, even the Bible arguably invites conjecture in its listing of demon possession alongside various other physical and mental illnesses (Matt 4:24). Certainly some of the symptoms appear to be treatable by modern medicine. But at the end of the day, if demons are real, they cannot simply be zapped away by a dose of anti-psychotic drugs. Even much of the medical community no longer equates demonism with epilepsy.[1] Naturally, the secular world still remains sceptical. If demons are real, life-altering action is required. Yet no one is comfortable with change. The scientific mind does all within its means to avoid an imminent cognitive dissonance. At a certain level the empire of scientific thought is founded upon quasi-religious principles of faith seldom attendant upon truth. A serious invitation to criticism or openness to a falsification of their claims, by means of a long awaited dialogue with the reputable religious community, is simply too dangerous a risk to take. As things stand, Christian believers are outliers. Their scholarly research is written off as paraphernalia while secularized "scientific" theory is blindly embraced as fact. Although truth is not contingent upon majority rule, the post-structuralist reprehension—that reality is at least partially a product of social construct—is applicable to this deteriorating arena of "academic" discourse. Although the platitudes of the secular world insinuate that the Christian Church is delusional, blurring the distinction between fantasy and reality is a rapidly-spreading problematic among the unbelieving populace.

The Church Fathers help us understand why the world is, literally, so confused. One cannot safely set out on a journey without a reliable map. Such a map is based on an accurate reading of reality. Most unbelievers are materialists. By denying the existence of the spiritual realm as entirely different from the physical one, the way they reason follows a fallacious map of a fictional land which, in turn, informs their distorted worldview. In contrast, the Christian map incorporates both the visible and invisible planes of reality. St. Augustine, one of the most important Fathers of the Western Church, organized these spiritual and earthly realities under the respective categories of the "City of God" and the "Earthly City," while investigating the implications of the overlap between them. This distinction

---

1. Despite many of its secular presuppositions, the medical community is increasingly recognizing the necessity of spiritual care alongside psychiatric treatment of those exhibiting alleged signs of demon possession. Koenig, *Faith and Mental Health*, 153.

Prologue

between these two realms furnishes Christianity's ability to interpret the human experience in accordance with a dual-lensed spectacle of the "two cities." In contrast, the secular world filters phenomena through a single-lensed epistemological hermeneutic informed by a metaphysic of the "one city." Reasoning through this "single-city" logic is inherently demonic because it collapses God-given distinctions. For instance, the ability to judge moral events by a higher or "heavenly" standard is diabolically perverted by the absence of a meaningful ethical grid. We encounter examples of this inability to critically evaluate cultural norms throughout any given day. For example, most traffic jams are caused by an endless line up of curious bystanders determined to observe the damage of a traffic accident. Is the rubbernecking altruistic? In other words, do drivers slow down in order to determine how they can be of some philanthropic assistance or do they do so because of a grotesque interest or even a sadistic desire—albeit subconscious? For the vast majority of our desensitized population, the unspoken feeling on the matter runs something like, "It's a free show—what's the problem?" Reality-TV stars are the new gladiators in the coliseum of our living rooms. The Romans catered no ethical dilemmas either. What compels an individual to prioritize videotaping their pending consumption by a hurricane or Tsunami over their own physical security? Television watching is indisputably harmless, right? Perhaps, unconsciously, we believe that placing a photo lens between the threat and our cornea provides the same protection. "How could my life possibly be endangered in the middle of a tweet!" the tourist protests as he is engulfed by an enormous wave. Not only do we blindly trust our media, but we unwarily depend on their mediums as our authorities—and so they become our gods. The objectification of the female and male form warps the ability to realistically evaluate the beauty of one's spouse. We tithe an unsettling amount of our income to the image of a billboard in pathetic attempts at approximating our aesthetic qualities to a plastic prototype or a Hollywood star that has just undergone another series of futile face-lifts. Beauty is not in the eyes of the beholder but in the eyes of the culture. And yet the archetype is a fake and a lie. A critical approach to advertisements is driven by the awareness of our interaction with an artificial reality. The goal of most ads is to breed covetousness. They rarely fulfill our needs. Usually they stealthily create *wants* and then trick us into believing that we have always *needed* them.

Navigating safely through this dangerous spiritual labyrinth of temptation, vanity and conflicting desires and intuitions is vital for Christians who claim to be counter-cultural disciples of the cross. Godly judgments require sharpening through prayer and study of God's Word since the domineering single-city logic inhibits one's ability to carefully distinguish between differing realities. For those who view the world along that single and simple plane, appellations, demons and spirits, if they exist at all, must be recordable on radiation detectors and other physical apparatus. For them, it is unfathomable to envision even spiritual bodies as belonging to some other sphere besides the earthly one with which we are all fully familiar. Given these presuppositions reincarnation makes some sense. Like our bodies, our souls remain trapped within the single-planed bubble of temporal reality. So, too, some Christians insist that souls have mass.

If the veins in your brain are presently pulsating, that's a good sign. Thinking deep sometimes hurts. However, allow me one further illustration to clarify the strenuous point. As a chaplain deployed to the Middle East, I remember peering through a set of binoculars with a few sentry guards from the top of a cliff. Even though we were participating in a surveillance of enemy territory, the landscape was spine-tinglingly beautiful. The fantastic feeling that people often have when fixing their eyes on a desirable object was immediately interrupted by a disturbing crunching sound underneath the soles of my combat boots. When I looked down below my feet, it quickly became apparent that I was stepping on some bones—human bones! As a matter of fact, I was standing in the midst of a skeletal rib cage. Widening the perimeter of my vantage point, I noticed that not only was I standing on a few, I was surrounded by an endless sea of bones mixed with sand, dust and rubble. The entire hill appeared to have consisted of human bones.[2] Tripping over a chunk of skull, I was inclined to join with Dorothy's observation after arriving into the Land of Oz: "I've a feeling we're not in Kansas anymore." Ezekiel had a vision of a valley of dry bones. Here I was standing on a mountain of them! The Church operates within the presumption that there are two planes to reality.[3] Yet only those who turn their heads can clearly see with this double vision. St. Augustine would call that "conversion." Most non-Christians are myopic. They tend

---

2. Although it is hard to tell, since cadavers were often buried in unmarked shallow desert graves, the mountain was likely a mass grave for which enemy forces were responsible.

3. Although there is an overlap between temporal and eternal realities in what many call "spirituality" (for Christians, prayer, liturgy and sacraments act as links between the two spheres), the rules that function within one sphere do not necessarily apply to the other.

Prologue

to view only a landscape and fail to perceive another simultaneous reality directly beneath them. Just like I had lost my footing in my hypnotic fixation, conducting one's life in neglect of this double-vision is sure to result in a tumultuous and unpredictable voyage. In Holy Baptism Christians receive a new lens that governs their lives, not only informing their moral compasses, but acting also as an internal GPS that allows them to better understand wider societal trends and chisel away at conventional wisdom.

One final example (I promise): on the one hand, spiritually-sensitive people today have heedlessly turned environmental sustainability into a pagan religion, paying homage to the pantheistic goddess "Mother Nature." The well-meaning ecological principles of this animistic worldview operate within a one-planed bubble of earthly phenomena. All future possibilities are contingent upon the survival of a measureable creation. On the other hand, the redneck types with bumper stickers stating "He with the most toys wins" deride recycling and salute acid rain. These two seemingly radically different worldviews are both hinged in the same demonic error. How both the immanence and transcendence of a personal God fit into a system in which a rudimentary distinction between the creation and the Creator has been tossed aside remains a challenge for the unenlightened unbeliever. With their "double-vision" Christians should be less prone to confusing realms and categories in interpreting the meaning of both the Holy Scriptures and the events of everyday life. It is to be expected that they be more open-minded to testimonies regarding the supernatural as well.

This leads me to the other reason that I am hesitant to talk about my experiences. I want to avoid sensationalizing them. The Holy Scriptures are relatively silent on the topic of demons. We know a great deal more about the good angels than we do about the bad ones. And so should it be, lest our curiosity be roused to unbiblical exertions and sacrilege. To God alone be the glory. However, we are given a few clues about the fallen angels and clear instructions as to how to rid ourselves of them. The writings of the Church Fathers and ancient liturgies can help us. I am not so pretentious as to equate my contribution with theirs. To the contrary, I pray that I would stay clear of speaking beyond those things permitted by the Holy Scriptures, distracting a listener from the voice of our dear Lord and mighty Master Jesus Christ. I only hope that I have composed some meaningful thoughts woven together in synchronized conformity with solemn logic, Christian tradition and the Word of God—and that all of them are lacking in originality.

My First Exorcism

Outside of Roman Catholicism, there is a surprisingly little amount of credible material on the tactical considerations with regards to exorcism and a ministry of deliverance from the wide spectrum of demonic activity to which we are exposed.[4] It would appear that the Reformation churches of the sixteenth-century were so busy preserving the priceless jewel of the doctrine of justification—*sola fides* and *solus Christus*—that some of the other precious treasures of the Church had become neglected. Lutherans may lack resources, but they add an integral component to the conversation. Namely, belief in the assurance of salvation delivered to believers by Christ through Holy Baptism is an integral prerequisite before engaging in demonic combat, since the devil's most effective weapon is to cast doubt upon the competencies of our General and Lord and have us question our status as His subordinates and His children. My hope is that my narrative-based introduction to the topic will trigger a desire in exploring and rediscovering—and even, dare I say, *developing*—material, tools and resources for the Church at large.

Over the years I have come to realize that I have had an unusually high number of encounters with demons. I have witnessed bizarre and disturbing things that I hope never to see again. I share some of them here. Many of my brothers in the ministry have never experienced anything similar. I remember asking a seminary professor why candidates for the holy ministry received so little training on exorcism. It was indicated to me that such encounters for clergy were rare in the developed world. There is some truth in this. Whereas the portfolios of overseas missionaries are saturated with stories of exorcisms, the devil finds it less advantageous to be overly obvious in a secular, modern, and largely agnostic or atheistic culture. Demonic presence only confirms the existence of the spiritual realm. In the under-developed countries the existence of God is presupposed. In poverty-stricken regions the question becomes, "Which are stronger, the evil forces or the good ones?" Religious people guess as to the allegiance that offers more temporal advantages. Fellow workers in the ministry are quite accustomed to demon possession in places such as Haiti or Western Africa. But even in North America, one should be well-equipped.

Personally, I believe that I have encountered demon possession in at least three known individuals to whom I ministered Christ's Word and

---

4. For more information on the role of exorcism in the Lutheran tradition, see Robert H. Bennett who concisely explores the contributions of Martin Luther, C.F.W. Walther and Francis Pieper, to name a few, in *I Am not Afraid*, 129–167.

Sacraments. The reason that I say "known" is because it is not always clear as to who is "possessed" and who is "oppressed," and to what degree. There is a difference. Without going into great detail, stages of diabolical influence may also include subjugation, infestation and affectation.[5] Certainly, each and every Christian is daily targeted by the evil fiend in thought, word and deed. The Old Adam abides alongside the New until the Christian enters Glory, and a return to one's baptism is nothing other than a constant drowning of that evil foe and his influence in the holy blood of Jesus. In this sense, every baptism is a "baptism of blood," just not our own. Moreover, every baptism is a kind of exorcism, since we are born children of the devil and are made into children of God (1 John 3:10). In the case of children, sponsors rebuke Satan on behalf of the speechless infant who is unable to articulate his faith himself. In the ancient Greek tradition, godparents would literally spit at the devil as they turned away from the font. Whether a child or adult, we are transferred from the Babylonian kingdom of darkness to the heavenly kingdom of light, as pronounced in the holy liturgy: "Depart from <u>name</u>, you unclean spirit, and make way for the Holy Spirit, in the name of the Father and of the Son and of the Holy Spirit. Amen."[6] Henceforth, baptized believing Christians are born again. The evil hound may still bark at us but he retains no bite due to Christ's propitiating atonement for us on the cross; a victory delivered to us in those "rosy-red" waters of Holy Baptism, as Martin Luther coined so well.[7] It is an appropriate detail that the pigs into which Jesus cast the demons were drowned *in water* (Matt 8:28–34). The Old Man and our sins are drowned too. Therefore Christians treat the devil with contempt. Well aware that we refuse to love him, he hopes at the very least that we fear him. Yet Christians need not be afraid, if they stand guard by hiding within Christ our fortress (Ps 18:2).

Demonic oppression and possession ensnare those who unwittingly expose themselves to the enemy's malevolent community. Sometimes there is an implicit or explicit request that the Holy Spirit step aside as the evil one is invited to take His place as part and parcel of apostasy from the Christian Faith.[8] At other times, the Holy Spirit is not present at the start. In any case, normally this dark dialogue occurs through various levels of contact with

---

5. Amorth, *An Exorcist tells his Story*, 79.

6. From Dr. Martin Luther's 1526 rite in *Rites and Resources for Pastoral Care*, 143.

7. AE 51: 325

8. Accordingly C.F.W. Walther mentions how the "devout" can also be possessed by demons. *Walther's Pastorale*, 214.

the occult and black magic. Although professionally trained exorcists claim that some may be the passive recipients of curses, spells, blood pacts, black magic, or witchcraft—even through spiritual ailments rooted in the family since childhood (i.e. "guilt by association")[9]—all demonically oppressed or possessed individuals with whom I, personally, have interacted have willingly permitted themselves contact with the occult. *Demonic oppression* can be tackled with fasting and prayer for God's release coupled with a faithful study and hearing of God's holy Word. Yet *demon possession* often requires the more severe treatment of a scheduled exorcism which both commands and binds the demon with the word and power of Christ which compels it.[10] The demon is ordered to discontinue its harm and return to its source—forever. Although Christians are never called to engage in exotic demon-chasing crusades, but should "stand guard"[11] in the spots where God has placed them (Eph 6:10–20)—the demons hunt us on our terrain obviating all human expeditions into theirs—in the case of a demoniac the demon is invoked, rebuked and expelled. Of course, it is never our prayers, but those of our valiant champion that pulverize these hostile enemy forces.

When reading the New Testament, one gets the impression that the demon-possessed were always clearly so: tied up in chains, banished into the desert, etc. But in my experience, demons can remain hidden for extensive periods of time inside their host, influencing their behaviour, haunting their thoughts, playing with their souls, and only periodically manifesting their presence publicly. One of the demoniacs with whom I worked could summon her demon at will. Because demons like to hide, some of them need to be coaxed or goaded out through lengthy prayers and precise commands. Evidently, there are various degrees of demonic activity. Each case demands a unique pastoral response.

Naturally, the content of this book may not be suitable for all readers. Some will find the narratives daunting, while for others the more austere components of certain commentaries may prove unsettling. Notwithstanding the title, this book is not about exorcism. A disquisition indubitably resembling a diatribe at times, the accounts of demonic oppression and possession recorded here offer a springboard intended to stimulate critical thinking, challenge metaphysical presuppositions and inspire belated conversation on a series of topics that have traditionally been avoided due

---

9. Amorth, *An Exorcist: More Stories*, 138; Vogl, *Begone Satan!*, 19.
10. Amorth, *An Exorcist*, 25–52.
11. See John W. Kleinig, *Grace upon Grace: Spirituality for Today*, 256–260.

to the impetuosity that they incite inside each one of us. Advancing no succinct plot, these streams of thought delineate inquiries into the subtleties of demonic activity of individual and communal life as their common thread. Furthermore, the opinions expressed herein are in no way representative of the military institution for which I work, nor are they reflective of all the clergy within my church body. But more than likely it is the subject matter and eyewitness accounts that will be deemed most disturbing. St. John Chrysostom likened the practice of biblical hermeneutics to sea travel in which some, who are less accustomed to it, experience seasickness. The dizziness felt arises not from the sea, but rather from the voyagers' inexperience at sea.[12] The analogy may be applicable to this odyssey. In any case, let us now leave the harbor and enter the depths together.

> Jacob's Star in all its splendor,
> Beams with comfort sweet and tender,
> Forcing Satan to surrender,
> Breaking all the powers of hell.[13]

---

12. Chrysostom, *Old Testament Homilies*, 8.
13. TLH 90.

A Midsummer's Nightmare

> That evening they brought to him many who were oppressed by demons, and he cast out the spirits with a word and healed all who were sick. (Matt 8:16)

If there were a list of the top 10 things not to do while exorcizing a demon, one of the first would read: "Have a conversation with it." Though I made many others, that mistake was not one of them. I was, however, tempted. I will explain later.

I was nineteen years of age when I first heard a devil speak. I befriended a classmate, who had survived a life of various kinds of abuse, coupled with a wide range of experimentation with illegal drugs and accented by regular forays into the satanic arts. I have given her the pseudonym "Lisa." I suspected that she was not altogether normal by her occasional zone-outs in which she would fall into a seeming trance. Her eyes would tenuously fog over as she deafened herself to my voice. An aura of concentration would overtake her facial expression as if she were listening to another speaker, even though we were alone. It was my first exposure to this kind of parapsychological phenomena. An acquaintance of mine displayed almost identical behaviour. He too was involved in the occult. In both cases, the episodes did not last more than a minute and the victim had no recollection of what had just transpired.

There was no question in my mind that these individuals were oppressed by something demonic. The peculiar displays were distressing, but I had no doubts that Jesus Christ was victorious over the devil and his evil hosts. One collect for Easter boldly states how by His death on the cross and His glorious resurrection we have been delivered from the enemy camp rendering all of Satan's power ineffectual. Confirmed in the Lutheran

Church, I full-heartedly believed that every Christian had the authority and power to rebuke the evil tyrant, and this included counteracting his physical manifestations. Even at a young age we learned about the implications of the "communication of attributes" from the divine nature to the human nature of Christ. The word "Christology" may not have been uttered in our Sunday school class, but the notion was presupposed even in pre-adolescence. Derived from the logic of an early church council at Chalcedon in AD 451, the *genus maiestaticum* summarizes how the divine attributes are delivered to the human nature of the person of Christ due to its personal union with His divinity. This theological language may seem esoteric to the laity, but when one patiently unpacks the concepts and reverently reflects upon their elating claims, even the simplest child is filled with both mesmerizing awe and heart-warming comfort. Jesus' divine Word, deployed from human lips, stills storms. Wow! Due to the incarnation, the powers of God are not locked away in heaven. They have vanished from human sight but are still actively expressed through physical means. For instance, after His resurrection, the man Jesus passes through locked doors. He is witnessed appearing and disappearing. These are properties reserved for spirits. Yet Jesus is not a ghost. He is a man, and remains a man. In order to defuse their doubts, the Lord chooses to eat with His disciples. He does the same today as His omnipresence continues to be employed by means of His human nature. He remains present in the flesh of His body and blood through Eucharistic celebrations at all times and at all places. He is always fully, and not partially, with us. The grip of evil may oscillate, but the presence of God never fluctuates. His nearness is not a yo-yo contingent upon our shifting prayers or lack of holy inner qualities. He is a God who has become man, *entirely*. He remains fully human—yet mostly hidden. The birth of Christ, which assumed all flesh in Himself, and His subsequent redemptive works culminating on Good Friday has re-dignified our human nature in general and our Christian bodies in particular. We are, after all, *His* body. Hence, those divine attributes and powers are, in a mystical and mysterious sense, our possession. *My* words can now frighten the demons by both form and content: they protrude from fleshly lips redeemed by Christ, the God-man, and they carry a divine message originating in the heavenly city. When God made humankind in His image, He knew that one day He would assume that very image in its entirety by the virgin birth.

I sometimes wonder whether or not the devil is jealous that God did not assume the form of an angel. In C.S. Lewis' science-fiction novel, *Out of the Silent Planet*, the aliens on other planets (who also worship the Triune God) are dumbfounded and bewildered in their first meeting with a human being. Here before them stood the unique creature whose form the boundless Creator of the universe had assumed! God became man! The Creator had incorporated human beings into His life and Being. The authority that belonged to Christ had been communicated to His people and, to some extent, so had His capabilities.

That being said, what I didn't know then but do know now, is that the "priesthood of all believers" doesn't qualify every Christian to do all the same works in all the same places and at all the same times. Every part of Christ's body battles the devil to different degrees, and to ignore distinctions between members is a very dangerous business indeed. Roman Catholic canon law forbids the laity any use of formulas of exorcism or their corresponding sacramentals (e.g. exorcized salt, oil and water). The exorcists undergo professional training. Even those who possess a certain *charisma* or gift of sensitivity for detecting demonic presence (and deciphering diabolical possession from, say, psychological illness) must have a reputation for being humble, prayerful and rejecters of money and theatrics, before they are publicly acknowledged and commissioned.[1] Although we may find some of these restrictions legalistic, one must never forget that an exorcist acts on behalf of the Church at large—the Church militant—and not as an individual. For the same reason, the catholic and apostolic Church has authorized only ordained priests to preside over the mass and only divinely called pastors to preach publicly. When lay people attempt demonic warfare in a non-transparent and private manner, they deprive themselves of the full power and capacity offered by the Church universal. "If all were a single member, where would the body be?" (1 Cor 12:19) This happened to be my error with Lisa.

+ + +

Lisa fell into one of her trances as we strolled out of her mother's dilapidated bungalow and passed in front of the weathered garage door. It was mid-summer, early afternoon. After a few steps, she froze in a stupor, except for her arms that swayed at her sides like rubber bands. Standing still as a mannequin, her head fell forward, motionless. This time, in this trance, something was different. She was not herself. More accurately, she was not

---

1. Amorth, *More Stories*, 162.

there at all—something else was. I stepped away from her and asked God for guidance through a very short prayer with my eyes wide open. I had nothing to lose. I felt a bit paranoid, especially if it all turned out to be an immature prank. I began to address—what I thought might be—a demon. A wave of terror swept over me and I broke into a cold sweat. It all seemed so surreal. Lisa started to tremble slightly, head still hanging low, her face hidden under a veil of thick dark hair masking her sinking frame. To my surprise, I heard a deep voice protrude from a mouth that normally produced a high-pitched tone. It stated simply, "she's mine," after which the host resumed her ordinary state. No foaming at the mouth or 360 degree head spins. Yet those two simple words spoken in the third person sent chills up my spine. What an accurate expression summarizing its possession: "she's mine." It turned out that it was right.

St. Augustine, who is one of the first Christians to develop a formalized "demonology," describes demons as discontented entities. Despising their creaturely status and envying human beings, they seek to enter human bodies and take residence therein, like a thief breaking into a house. Their ability to succeed is partially determined by whether or not the owner has left the door unlocked, or even left it swung wide open in an inviting manner. Actually "demon possession" is etymologically misrepresentative. Satan can never "possess" anything entirely (at best he can "borrow") since the one true God remains the giver of all things. He alone retains the exclusive title of "Maker." In the end, it is the devil's greatest frustration.[2] He remains a creature in spite of his ambition to become the Creator. Even hell is not under his rule. There, he suffers worse than all. In short, the demons feel themselves to be unfulfilled, dissatisfied with their place in life, driving them to usurp that of other creatures.[3] But no matter where they are or what they do, they will never abide in joy. It sounds all too familiar. We too share in this error in our unhappiness with regards to *our* stations in life: jealous of our neighbours' success or vocations, wife or husband, home, children, and whatever else belongs to him or her. We fraternize with

---

2 As a father I consider it a great honour to form, mold and shape the lives of my children. The wonderful vocation of parenthood allows me to participate in the incredible creative energies of God. While most parents aim to lovingly raise these gifts with which they have been entrusted, assuring that they grow well, the devil seeks only to contort, bend and destroy whatever he happens to possess at any particular moment. In short, the devil's "creative" energies do not *form*, but rather *deform*, revealing the great difference between him and his creator, aggravating and inflaming his wicked frustration.

3. *City of God*, VIII: 16–17.

the league of demons in our nebulous longing for membership in a more "suitable" church, life in a flashier city, the salary of a more lucrative job paired with a more exalted position, and all the other sins against the last commandments. We unobtrusively grumble, "If only I was God, I would do things differently." Lucifer shared this same sentiment even before our creation.

+ + +

The nature of a demon is a subject worth pondering. The word "demon" comes from the Greek *daimon*, which can be translated as "instrument" or "tool." Ironically, demons do not want to *be* what they *are*. Loathing their instrumentality, they reject their place in the cosmological hierarchy. Our Lord warns, "When you see the abomination of desolation standing where he ought not to be (let the reader understand), then let those who are in Judea flee to the mountains" (Mark 13:14). Unlike their angelic brothers, they refuse to remain God's messengers and helpers, taking residence in places to which they are not assigned. Along with punk rock star Iggy Pop, they "lust for life," but not their own. They want ours. Like us human beings, they are dissatisfied with their position in life. They reject their identity as servants and wish to seize the place of the king. They abhor being "used" and lust to be "ends," even though that unique position is already fulfilled by God Himself who is the single end of all things.

The Lord is the sole source of peace, rest, love, and joy although the demons adamantly deny it (while we often resist it). Accordingly, every creature's fulfilment is uniquely in Him. Even unbelievers know this to be true intuitively. The secular world too has its prophets. The novels of Henry James and Ernest Hemingway impart a message that all human choices lead to dissatisfaction. A disproportionate number of poets commit suicide. True peace and rest for the Christian are found solely in God because, at the end of the day, at the end of our life, at the end of the world, we have one single use. Just as a light bulb finds satisfaction solely in an electrical socket, having no other use, so too, worship is the manner in which human beings are plugged into God, their unique source of eternal contentment. But due to our sinful and corrupt nature we have allied ourselves with the devil, a false plug and empty hole: the begetter of death, robber of life, root of all evil and vice, instigator of envy, font of avarice, fomenter of discord, and author of all pain and sorrow. We are clueless to the fact that our simple dissatisfactions betray our true allegiance. Yet just like the demons, *we* do not want to be what *we* are. Notwithstanding our identity as children of light we are all too easily attracted to the shadows and the darkness. The rhetoric of human servanthood and instrumentality rings inherently offensive, suggesting images of oppression by eighteenth-century slave drivers mistreating their human property. Characteristic of the demonic is scorn of one's true identity and spurn of one's place and role in God's order. Accordingly, demons are riotous monsters of chaos. In the Eastern Church sin is not described in terms of a deliberate wilful opposition to God. Instead, the sinful nature is framed within a discourse of man's inability to know himself and God clearly: a confusion of identity. During one exorcism, a demon was quoted describing hell in the following way:

> Everyone lives folded within himself and torn apart by his regrets. There is no relationship with anyone; everyone finds himself in the most profound solitude and desperately weeps for the evil that he has committed.[4]

For creatures that find their satisfaction, fulfilment and peace in something that lies outside of their own personhood, hell is the absolute expression of navel-gazing—useless.

According to St. Augustine, demons are restless and confused creatures. Therefore, they never enjoy peace. To put things very mildly, they are like spoiled bratty children who don't get their way and throw a tantrum— for eternity. Still, they remain more powerful and clever than a neighbourhood bully, devoting themselves to pulling the rest of God's creation into their self-created misery. Their followers are residents of "Babylon," Hebrew for "confusion." Augustine's *City of God* summarizes the demonic error as a mixing up of "use" with "enjoyment" which occurs through the confusion of all orders in life.[5] For example, an anti-rational society steered by sensation and hyper-romance is apt to confuse ontological distinctions essential to the maintenance of healthy relationships. There are four distinctive words for 'love' in Greek. English has collapsed them all into one, with grave consequences. What is bestiality or pedophilia other than a confusion of *philia* (friendship) or *storge* (affection) with *eros*, from which we obtain the word "erotic"? Defenders of these perversions are, nevertheless, sincere. The discipline of economics stresses how the stock market is only as stable

---

4. Amorth, *An Exorcist*, 76.
5. *City of God*, XIV: 27–28; XIX: 13.

as it is perceived to be. Reality becomes anecdotal to the truth. Feelings and perceptions are mutually dependent. They can both be sincere, but still misplaced. Demons are fixated on muddling up and confusing God's order through their relentless pursuit of turning our love for the Creator (*agape*) towards creation, with the result of devising new gods in our own image.

The Augustinian monk, Martin Luther, would later apply this theorem to pastoral care. Specifically, he accentuated how the mixing up of theological concepts and their implicit orders, such as the fundamental differences between things pertaining to the realm of Law and those of the Gospel (i.e. confusing the commands and promises of God), was evil and harmful.[6] Confusing the letter that kills with the spirit that gives life is spiritual suicide (2 Cor 3:6). Accordingly, the God-fearing navigator fluctuates between the poles of what we ought to do but are unable, and what Christ has done on our behalf and in our stead. For example, the question regarding what "Jesus would do" in any particular moral instance provides little guidance in the cogitations of our ethical decision-making. Routinely boycotting a company's products because of their link to abuse in the developing world presumes the existence of morally uncontaminated multinationals. How do our political alliances shift when Palestinian Christians outnumber Messianic Jews? Moreover, innocent children huddle *on both sides* of barbed-wire fences, regarded by armies as potential adults and eventual threats. We live interdependently with a corrupted global network paralyzing all ability to react in a holy manner. I am not perfect. I am also not the invincible holy Son of God. This does not excuse me to do the wrong thing but offers a compelling explanation for the limits of doing the right thing. Because of the poisonous repercussions of the fall from Eden, all of one's good moral behaviour is perverted to some extent. A work may still be good (as all good deeds arising from a Christian heart—as saint, not as sinner—are labelled fruits of God's Holy Spirit), but my motives are never entirely pure. The Old Adam remains within me until death. My deeds are not the problem; I am. I can give a magnanimous contribution to a charity, and it will likely do much good objectively. Yet some of my motivations are selfish. My generous donation may make me feel good, may demonstrate my importance at making a global difference, may assuage guilt, might provide

---

6. For a deeper exploration of Luther's view on confusions within theological logic as inherently demonic and how maintaining a proper distinction between the two spheres of eternal and temporal realities is a participation in spiritual war see Harold Ristau's *Understanding Martin Luther's Demonological Rhetoric in His Treatise Against the Heavenly Prophets (1525): How What Luther Speaks Is Essential to What Luther Says.*

proof that I am better than someone else, etc. *Lex semper accusat*: the Law always accuses us of our sin, exposing our inadequacy even with regards to our best attempts at fulfilling a divine rule. Evil stems from the corrupt heart. Where does that leave us? We are left with a great hope: naked and eager receptors of the Good News. The Gospel forgives our sins, exonerates our wrongs, and covers our unrighteousness with the merits of Christ. The Law has been fulfilled by Him, but credited to us. Some call this "imputed righteousness." Man is pure, not because of what he has done, but because of what has been done unto him. It terrifies all the hordes of hell, who may laugh at man's efforts to behave purely but now lay vanquished before the works of Jesus Christ.

Distracting man from this wonderful and life-altering Gospel announcement is an archetypal strategy for Satan. Demonic confusion penetrates our belief system when we think that our forgiveness is conditional on our works of the Law. It annuls a justification by grace through faith, which is the foundational doctrine to Christ's holy Church. Nothing pleases the devil more than believers convinced that they are saved by their works and not by grace alone. Eastern Christians disapprove of a Lutheran hermeneutic that dichotomizes faith and works, and even accuse it of subsiding incongruously with church history and the New Testament. Although Lutherans believe that salvation is *by* faith alone, they do not believe that it is by a faith that *is* alone. Yet, the theological distinction must be maintained. Otherwise, a treacherous merging of the quintessential doctrine of justification with sanctification occurs, partially pinning the assurance of the believer's saintly status in his or her own holiness as opposed to Christ's. Jesus Christ has clothed Himself with our sins, while we have dressed ourselves with His mantle of righteousness. The devil schemes to "cross-dress" these gowns. Some Eastern Orthodox who find the Lutheran fixation on the Second Person of the Holy Trinity to be slightly unbalanced, also discover St. Paul to be too "judicious" in his perception of the atonement. Nevertheless, the dialogue of life is permeated with dichotomies. The tension and friction intrinsic to our daily experiences of sin and grace, justice and mercy, and Law and Gospel are the uneven cobble stones beneath the war-torn feet of the human venture, a yin-yang that shapes our individual paths. There are multifarious ways to articulate the dichotomous relationship within the paradox while still remaining faithful to the dialectic. But when the two notions are twisted apart, mixed together or interchanged, the devil has achieved his ultimate goal.

Yet demonic confusion is not limited to individual human experience. Martin Luther observed the same kinds of confusions in the socio-political spheres, between the Two Kingdoms—God's rule on earth through both the instruments of the Church and those of the government. For example, the religious crusades were guilty of the same demonic error as the Social Gospel is today. They were attempts at turning temporal realities into eternal realities, or eternalizing temporal ones. Constantine's objective of erecting the first "Christian state" resembled the same thinking patterns of his contemporary pagans, despite his good intentions. All theocracies seek to materialize heavenly realities on earth. Although some of the crusades were politically motivated and even justifiable considering the threat of Islamic expansion, others were clearly driven by a view of spiritual conquest. Conquering the Holy Land embodied a physical victory over the spiritual dark forces. Still today, the Vatican is not just a church, but a state. The issue lies deeper than a cynical mixing of politics and religion, but exemplifies how easily the tools that belong to one realm can be mistakenly applied for use in the other. Years later, emerging from his exile at the Wartburg castle, Martin Luther was horrified to discover that his colleague Andreas Bodenstein von Karlstadt, in an effort to crush what he believed to be the worship of idols, had begun a rampage breaking all religious images, stained glass and statues of the saints. Luther rebuked him not only for demonically confusing the realms of inward cleanliness through such abominable outward behaviour, but also blamed him for the evil results: the unleashing of the Peasants' Revolt of 1524, an anarchistic and bombastic crusade against all authorities, both secular and religious, as a means for the lower classes to 'upgrade' their stations in life.

Political theorist Michael Waltzer addresses this phenomenon in his book *Spheres of Justice: A Defense of Pluralism and Equality*, arguing that the use of the instruments of one sphere in the other is the source of all acts of injustice. For example, during the inquisition, the physical sword was enlisted to drive out heresies even though doctrinal disputes ought to have been fought with the spiritual sword of the Word of God. The inquisition was well-intentioned: torturing and murdering the body in order to mitigate the more severe pains of purgatory. The confused use of physical methods to influence the spiritual realm is rooted in a skewed (i.e. demonic) anthropology with regards to the relationship between body and soul. Neo-Gnostic heresy—that one's bodily health reflects the status of one's soul[7]—yields many disciples and assumes various ill-boding epiphanies today. Although democracy should not determine church doctrine and practice, the importation of democratic principles from the kingdom of the Left to the Right[8] offers endless examples. Similarly, religious rhetoric does not cease to impregnate the kingdom of the Left. Democracy preaches that everyone is equal. Import this truism to the kingdom of the Right and everyone becomes a minister. Notwithstanding a spiritual equality between Christians through the "priesthood of all believers," any former distinctions between the laity and clergy become irretrievable. But are all people entitled to everything all the time and in all places? Most political revolutions, no matter how bloody, are hailed as inevitable due to the fact that they sought to assure liberty, justice and equal rights for all. It becomes unthinkable that a compassionate God would not bless a well-meaning revolt. The logic of the radical reformation reigns. Subordination, in all of its expressions is considered undemocratic. All forms of inequality observed in the Church, household, or society, are viewed with bitter vehemence. Demonic neo-Gnostic tendencies expressed through the modern feminist movement seek to overturn the order of creation and confuse it with the corollaries of the order of redemption, exposing the Church to the critique that it is, secretly, a misogynist institution. In accordance with this thinking, how can the Church be understood as anything other than sexist? Sexual organs are perceived as regrettable accidents of gender, providing no window into how men and women exist as different expressions of humanity. A feminization of gender is only one of the results of the demonic confusion between the Two Kingdoms.

In summary, demons remain messengers and servants, but of a master of their own crooked construction. Because they have strayed from the Truth and twisted the good, they are naturally liars and vindictive. Incidentally, because demons are liars, exorcists are even trained to limit the questions that they pose to them, lest they be manipulated by their lies. Some demons pretend to be holy angels, saints or the souls of the deceased. However, they are all deceivers and corrupters. Unsurprisingly, they are

---

7. Unlike the juncture between a created body and soul held within Christian anthropology, which necessitates kinds of physical means of grace to affect the spirit, the Gnostics either radically pitted the body and soul against each other or they collapsed them together: the body was either of utmost importance or maintained very little importance.

8. i.e. God's rule through secular authorities by the law to God's rule through His Church by His means of grace—the Gospel.

frustrated creatures, because, in spite of their resistance and sedition, they are still God's servants. Whether they like it or not, their creator still uses them for His divine purposes. Ironically, despite their reputation as rebels, the fallen angels remain God's slaves. The Holy Scriptures state how God permits the devil to test us (Rev 2:10) and purify us (1 Cor 5:5). Even St. Paul was afflicted with a thorn in the flesh, a "messenger from Satan," in order to keep him from "becoming conceited" (2 Cor 12:7). Evidently, Christians are also susceptible to demonic subjection. God uses His enemies for a greater purpose even though they may be unaware. The sufferings of Job, the sending of the angel of death in Egypt, the appointment of Judas, Caiaphas and all the calloused characters implicated in the crucifixion of our Lord exemplify both the Almighty's sovereignty, and His desire that, for those who love Him, all things work together for the good (Rom 8:28). Likewise Christ commands "Do not resist the one who is evil" (Matt 5:39). However unwillingly, the devil remains a tool in the hand of his Maker, echoed by the Church that still sings: "Satan you wicked one, own now your master."[9] Though forever dismissed from his prestigious position in the heavenly courts, the evil foe is unable to cease working for God as a slave. Thus, all his tactics against the faithful backfire with counterproductive results. Many of those once diabolically possessed confess an enriched relationship with God after their liberation. In fact, Dr. Martin Luther referred to the devil as the best teacher of theology,[10] because he drives despairing Christians to prayer and to the Holy Spirit. Like all Fathers of the Church Luther was not always right, but this concept expounds profound Christian genius. The devil cannot help but help us. By accusing us with the Law, God allows Lucifer to haul out the dark sinful critters and pests of our lives, only to be exterminated by the light radiating from our Saviour's blood-stained cross while their carcasses are swept away by the unending flood of grace flowing from His empty tomb. Defeated, yet full of frustrated rage, the devil continues to lash out against the friends of his enemies. But with no hope for a final victory, all of his efforts are desperate reactions enacted with a weathered and pathetic tail hanging between his legs.

---

9. LSB 533.
10. AE 54:50.

A Midsummer's Nightmare

+ + +

Humankind's banishment from the Garden of Eden may appear vindictive and evil at first: the act of an angry and malicious God. Yet Adam and Eve were not merely punished for committing some trivial wrong. Their poor decision-making has perilous implications for the destiny of all of us. They had broken off fellowship with God. Impure and unclean, God's holy presence became a dangerous one for these first humans and all of their descendants. So *God* decides to do something radical. *They* had done enough. Consistent with His fatherly instinct of cleaning up a child's mess, God exiles Adam and Eve from His garden—His table—for their own safety. He loves them so much that, against His very life-giving nature, He Himself heart-wrenchingly kills—sacrifices—one of the innocent beasts that He had just created in order to clothe them (I have a hunch that it was a lamb). Moreover, He curses the evil one and promises a saviour, as well as mercifully offering us His protective presence until our severed relationship with Him could finally be repaired on that first Good Friday. As strange as it may sound, God was compelled to hand us over to evil for our own good. For the Lord God said, "Behold, the man has become like one of us in knowing good and evil. Now, lest Adam reach out his hand and take also of the tree of life and eat, and live forever" (Gen 3:22), the King of kings excommunicated him from His royal garden. This consequential decision reflects the deepest of love, for the one tree gave access to the other. Had our Lord not taken these extreme and painful measures, we would have obliviously continued nourishing ourselves on the tree of life which would have immortalized our sinful state. Our "out-casting" delivered us from living eternity as sinners. Instead, we were rescued from ourselves and offered the antidote for our sin through the gift of Christ *via* the pill of Holy Baptism. By His cross we now have access once again to the tree of life, which immortalizes our saintly state when we eat of its fruits from the table of His holy altar. On the Last Day, when we behold God and the harvest of joy amassed from our sowing of tears, all tiring trials and agitating questions will disappear from memory, relinquishing their importance, as all things pure become absorbed in divine glorious beauty.

Although suffering is a divine tool and gift, which, when understood theologically, makes a lot of sense, the devil induces us to despise it by employing a "human reasoning" that Martin Luther rightly called "the devil's whore." While our logic deters us from embracing it— after all, everyone aspires to be on the winning team—suffering and God are a necessary unity which, alone, provide elementary shape and honest meaning to human existence. The impassibility of God does not preclude the fact that He still hurts, and His Spirit still grieves. Even if Christianity weren't true, it would still be the most enlightened religion. It uniquely resonates with the human condition, offering no beatific or idyllic vision of our depraved temporal existence. It boldly proclaims the unsinkable truth that we are, and remain, a broken race for which its creator suffers and dies. At the cross, God is emptied. His heart is pierced, drained, so that there would be room for us. Through the fountain of sweet water and the flood of quenching blood that spills from the Saviour's open side (John 19:34), the Holy Spirit draws all who suffer to Him who suffered for them. Though separately they bear on their aching bodies the still throbbing marks of Jesus' tender scars, together they rejoice in their common share in one holy mystical stigmata.

People who complain about a distant God who does not understand suffering need to be reminded that, remarkably, the very book He has authored includes incriminating material which, at first glance, seems to call into question God's love. The complaints of Job echo emotions that all people feel. Yet these divine self-disclosures are not recorded in the Bible in order to cast doubt upon the impeccably merciful character of God. Rather they demonstrate that our transcendent God is also immanent, and is well aware of our utmost feelings and frustration with suffering, sin, illness and death; that hidden beyond the recesses of time, is a meaning and information to which we have not necessarily been made privy. Job never becomes aware of the life lesson underlying his suffering. But we do. And his experience has acted as a source of comfort to innumerable believers since. Despite appearances of the diabolical, God Himself is present, shepherding His people into His kingdom. Consequently, the devil is the chief victim of his own traps. "When the devil kicks, he is struck," an Eastern patriarch once observed. Like each and every plan of Wile E. Coyote's to catch his arch-nemesis, the Road Runner, explodes in his face, the crucifixion is the tumultuous trigger and culmination of conquest within the cosmological dual. The Almighty had reduced Himself to a worm and not a man (Ps 22:6), a strategic manoeuvre in the activation of the final snare for the evil one. He becomes the bait on the hook of the cross, luring the devil to take a fatal bite. Sparing His wandering sheep from a destiny that we well deserve, Jesus, the Shepherd and the Lamb, fills the mouth of the hungry wolf with His own fiery flesh. Yet unable to swallow this hallowed unfamiliar meat,

A Midsummer's Nightmare

the beast chokes on his ultimate prize. He who once lured humankind in one garden by a poisonous fruit, is himself tempted to take and eat of a poisonous fruit, Jesus Christ who hangs on the tree of the cross in the garden of Calvary. After all, to some, the sacramental presence of our Lord's body brings life; to others, death (1 Cor 11:9). For this very reason, some exorcists carry a pyx containing the consecrated host to strike terror into the ancient dragon.

The Eastern Orthodox Church criticizes the imaginative similitudes of the economy of salvation, such as those imbibed from St. Anselm. The idea of God paying a ransom to the purging fires of hell or duping a fish all seem to diminish the sovereignty of God through inappropriate analogies of mythological semblance. Yet, although all human comparisons are naturally limited, such didactic metaphors and analogies offer ways of elucidating the unavoidable vicarious sacrifice required by an uncompromising system of justice put in place by God Himself. Both justice and grace are cheapened when theologians appeal to God's omnipotent ability to surpass the principles that He Himself has established through rhetorical questions such as "Can God create a rock heavier than He could lift?" Our God is not a showman, but rather a gentleman. He has honourably bound Himself to the same system in which He has established us. He is a general who fights alongside the troops on the battlefield and not from the headquarters in a distant country. If, however, the allegorical illustrations do represent the devil as having the upper hand, then that does convey its own incident of confusion.

+ + +

All incidents of confusion are, in a sense, demonic. It shouldn't have surprised me then that those frightening yet curious words "she's mine" from Lisa's lips were followed by a wild and exhausting month of demonic encounters and emotional chaos. My inexperience was betrayed in the creative methods I employed in attempting to free her of her satanic visitors, techniques largely learned from Hollywood movies and popular culture. My failure climaxed with her delirious attempt to throw herself out of a moving vehicle under the influence of the enemy. For the first time, the demon stared me in the eyes with cold spiteful darkened pupils of vexation, an image that I will carry with me to the grave. Amidst the falling ethereal darkness, a single lurid light beam from the passenger-side window coloured her progressively hardening face framing two gleaming empty holes. They were surging knives aspiring to pierce my innermost vulnerabilities. Repelled by this incredulous sneer and glance of scornful defiance, I grabbed her arm with a single-handed savage grip of desperation, while miraculously averting a collision with another vehicle. In the end, I dropped her off at an evangelical center that specialized in exorcisms with the hopes that they were less ill-equipped than I. It helped a bit. But the demons remained.

After further study of the topic in pursuit of some permanent solution, I eventually inquired into the status of Lisa's baptism. She told me that she was christened. "If she belonged to God, how could she remain possessed by an intruder?" I wondered. She seemed to honestly desire liberation. I was puzzled. Later I discovered that her pagan mother had baptized her in their upstairs bathtub after her birth because she didn't like organized religion. Did it count? Was it even Trinitarian? I am still unsure. The words do matter, more than one may believe. Some of us don't like to talk about a bad day at work, because it is like we are onerously reliving the irksome events—which were bad enough the first time around. The devil too hates hearing the Gospel story. But for him it is not just an astringent reminder. He actually relives his defeat again and again, for the "Word of God is living and active" (Heb 4:12).

I have often witnessed allegedly experienced pastors muddle up the Baptismal formula, "I baptize you in the name of the Father, and of the Son and of the Holy Spirit," causing me to seriously wonder about the presence of devilish hordes hidden from sight during the rite. They appear to direct all their energies to distract or jumble up the Spirit-inspired words, while the godparents are too enchanted by the cuteness of the little baby face and blinded by sentimentality, to notice the difference. After all, one of their primary roles as witnesses is to assure that the words spoken by the participants of the event are accurately delivered. Although easily memorisable, the words of the Trinitarian formula are unusually difficult to recount during the divine mystery of the moment, which is why I insist upon reading them—every single time! So the chance of an untrained lay unbeliever's attempt at successfully recreating a Christian baptism while sharing a bath with the candidate is pretty slim. In any case, nothing that I did seemed to help Lisa. Like many new believers who may find elements of the Christian faith an attractive means in helping them manage some personal issues, Lisa was only half-heartedly interested in resigning most of her frivolous addictions, including occult dabbling into the "deep secrets of Satan" (Rev 2:24). After all, the world tempts us to take control of our lives, while Jesus asks us to surrender them.

Witchcraft is an alluring tool to youth who feel themselves devoid of power or influence in their social networks. Eighteenth-century author Samuel Richardson expounds people's implicit inclination to abuse the weaker party, even when they themselves were once the underdog. Christians who indulge in the satanic arts are neither hot nor cold, but lukewarm in the faith; plants that spring-up quickly, but are choked away by the worries of life. I recently read in the newspaper that the "Santa Muerte" or "Saint Death" (represented by statues of the Grim Reaper) has recently made a come-back in Mexico, duping 10 million Catholics into worshipping him. Although banned by the Vatican, poverty-stricken followers willingly make pacts with this demon. He has a reputation for effectively delivering his part of the bargain, and expecting full payment for his services.[11] We all dream of speedy ways of achieving justice in accordance with our own terms and timings. Some are more desperate than others.

Lisa was desperate. But I was partly to blame as well. Although I was well-intentioned, I am not sure whether or not I aggravated the situation. Romantic feelings that developed over the course of a rather ephemeral relationship were certainly counterproductive, contributing to the eluding of vigilance and neglect of precaution. Yet it was my first unabashed exposure to anything resembling an exorcism, however unsuccessful.

> What harm can sin and death then do?
> The true God now abides with you.
> Let hell and Satan rage and chafe,
> Christ is your Brother—ye are safe.
>
> Not one He will or can forsake
> Who Him his confidence doth make.
> Let all his wiles the Tempter try,
> You may his utmost powers defy.[12]

---

11. At the same time, contracts with the devil can be broken. One Christian youngster was healed of her illness after a satanic pact was made and inscribed on a piece of paper that she carried around her neck in an amulet. After repentance, she was delivered from the demonic oppression even though her illness returned. She held no regrets. See Koch, *Occult Bondage and Deliverance*, 116.

12. TLH 103.

The Art of Exorcising

> But Jesus rebuked him, saying, "Be silent and come out of him!" And when the demon had thrown him down in their midst, he came out of him, having done him no harm. (Luke 4:35)

My first *successful* exorcism occurred while I was a parish pastor in an inner city church. Several of our members struggled with special impairments to their mental faculties, reflective of the surrounding neighbourhood. A healthy church ought to be a cross-section of the local population—whatever "healthy" happens to mean.

A lady who had a long history of sexual licentiousness and substance abuse randomly looked up our church in a phonebook. Because the name of our church started with an "A," we were naturally one of the first churches to be contacted by unchurched people looking for religious or spiritual services, whether it be funerals, weddings or, in this case, an exorcism. The individual, whom I have named "Debby," telephoned the parish office as a final desperate cry for help before deciding to terminate her life. She was spurred on by the aggressive advice of a multitude of unceasing voices in her head diminishing her ability to think clearly and choose responsibly. However, an entirely unfamiliar voice inclined her to seek out another opinion. I asked her if she had at all dabbled in the occult. With some hesitancy, and after an awkward silent pause, she answered in the affirmative. After she was convinced to choose life, I read some Scriptures to her and spoke some prayers. She thirsted for more. This oppressed soul had never been baptized and knew very little about the Christian faith.

Debby invited me to visit her at a government housing project located in a rundown neighbourhood of the city. The following day I visited her dingy apartment. The entrance reminded me slightly of the narthex of an orthodox church by the cloud of residual smoke that welcomed me. Yet, instead of the sweet-smelling aroma of incense, I was fumigated by the pungent odour of cheap cigarettes. The whole place reeked of death, depression and sadness. The bachelor unit was tiny, but functional. It was littered with ash-trays, drug paraphernalia, junk mail and coupons extracted from trashy magazines. Debby, an unkempt and very obese woman, ensconcing a ghastly pale face and bleak and fatigued eyes, appeared somewhat ashamed of the sepulchral tone of her living conditions. At the same time, there was a complacent aura about her while, accented by a flickering hopeless sigh, she guided me through the labyrinth of fast-food wrappers and busted furniture, escorting me to a place prepared on a foldout chair in the middle of the room.

After a short discussion, it became clear to me that, although *she* wanted me to stay, I was not welcome—by someone, or rather, by some*thing* else. As I continued to express God's word of forgiveness and tender compassion to her, sharing with her the Gospel story of the prodigal son and the heavenly Father's unconditional love even for the most sinful of individuals, she displayed an increasing difficulty in gazing me in the eyes. There was a sly, malicious twinkling in her eye. It glared at me with a frankness and confidence as from one superior to suspicion. The eyes, after all, are the window of the soul. At first, I assumed that she was resisting the Good News as some new converts do when they are utterly astonished by the superabundance of God's grace, and before they ecstatically devour the happy fact that they are accepted by a merciful Maker and are offered a new life with no further requirements on their part. Lamentably, others become fixated on their sins, and their shame prevents them from embracing the wonderful message. One task of the pastor is to decipher the difference.

Eventually Debby broke down in tears of exhilarating joy, or so I thought. Today I wonder if they were mixed with disingenuous drops of intimidation and even terror—and whether or not all of those tears were even Debby's! I gave her a Bible and some other Christian material, offered her a fatherly embrace with promises of ongoing support and an upcoming discussion on baptismal preparation. Although she said very little, she was genuinely sad to see me go.

A few days later, I received a phone call from Debby. It was another cry for aid. However, this time, I initially thought that I was a victim of a prank call. My senses detected only a heavy breathing, followed by deep nebulous moans and groans. Yet this was no sick joke. Suddenly, Debby whimpered something. It was unrecognizable; her natural voice was repeatedly interrupted by dark unnatural noises, bordering on growls, making it extremely difficult to determine what she was saying. Seconds later, something prohibited her from talking altogether. Although she remained on the phone listening intently, she said nothing. I continued to hear only a beastly breathing in the background, a memory that will likely follow me to my grave. As I read to her God's Word interjected by earnest supplications, the moans became more intense and defined. Finally, her own voice resurrected in a weak utterance: "help me." She hung up the receiver with a jerk. At that moment I realized that Debby was in danger. I was well aware of what those ungodly creatures are capable of doing, or rather, *persuading* us to do since, after all, I have all too often entertained them in the dark recesses of my own life. "God, be merciful to me, a sinner" (Luke 18:13b). But this time, it was not about me.

I immediately gathered my briefcase containing a stole, crucifix, communion kit, and anointing oil. I also grabbed my *Rites and Resources for Pastoral Care* from the Australian Lutheran Church which included some invaluable liturgical resources on dealing with spiritual oppression. On route, I called a clerical colleague and left a voicemail asking him—no, *begging* him—to accompany me on this visit by meeting me at her address. Feeling ill-equipped and inadequate, I hoped to God that I wouldn't have to face this disaster alone! The pastoral ministry is already marked by enough disappointment. But I was terrified of the irremediable consequences if this event followed suit. Lives were potentially at stake. Terror is an understatement. It was all horror and doom. I was a mediocre spiritual soldier, and an even less competent exorcist. My past exposure to the subject did not prepare me for this!

Yet there was profound comfort in my knowledge that a Christian's power over the unholy trinity of sin, death and the devil is not based on the strength of his or her personal faith. Rather the victory was already founded on God's concrete, holy and solid Word, embodied in the Christ event. We are assured in the Epistle to the Romans: "The God of peace will soon crush Satan under your feet. The grace of our Lord Jesus Christ be with you" (Rom 16:20). We have the choice to walk the bridge between man and God—a chasm overcome by the wood of the cross—in confidence *or* by testing each and every step. While both get us across, one offers a more peaceful trip. But in the end, it is the bridge itself, and not our ability to

The Art of Exorcising

walk, that preserves us. Even the spiritual hypochondriac makes it across. The size of our faith is often overvalued.

Even the alleged faith-healers must admit that their belief is publicly exposed as smaller than a mustard seed, since they have yet to move a mountain or even heal their own flu bugs for that matter. "Physician, heal yourself!" After all, the wages of sin is death, and we all die—even the showmen. At the same time, some of them are legitimate, which is why one must be careful judging a faith by its fruits (Matt 7:15-20). Even the unfaithful cast out demons in Jesus' name (Matt 7:22). Besides, the juiciest fruits are nourishing Christian doctrines. Televangelist Oral Roberts' instruction that viewers seeking a quick cure to their illness place a cup of water on the television box and drink it afterwards is more in tune with mediumistic healing than anything Biblical.[1] Just because something works doesn't mean that it is good. Christian evangelists may not even be aware that they are instruments of the devil. The Anti-Christ of the Apocalypse is a pretend Christian and his servants perform legitimate miracles (Rev 16:14). Demoniacs frequently possess unusual, even superhuman, strength (Mark 5:3). Clearly the devil is able to cause healing and injury and not just mimic them. The magicians competing with Moses did not just perform alleged tricks (Ex 7-8). There are even rumours of the devil raising the dead—temporarily. One Christian missionary records a famous Shaman of an Inuit tribe who was able to raise the heathen from the dead, although he lost this power after his conversion to Christianity.[2] Modern magicians claim these abilities as well. If they are real, it is certainly due to occult influence. Those who experience such healings are sure to endure enormous burdens as well.[3] In 2013, the well-known magician, Criss Angel, publicized a controversial magic trick which entailed attaching a corpse to a breathing apparatus which apparently resuscitated the deceased. He simultaneously placed a volunteer in a hypnotic state who then communicated with the dead. It was a compelling video. *Youtube* wouldn't lie—would it?

---

1. Koch 55.

2. Ibid 22. Koch also records how some aboriginals in Australia, after their conversion to Christianity, lost their telepathic communicative ability to speak with the dead; although some continued to receive the occasional unwelcome conversations from close relatives. Koch 41.

3. Bennett 61. Similarly, occasionally the enemy speaks the truth, whether it be through demons, fortune-tellers or other dark means. However, it is always intended to jeopardize God's will (See Acts 16:16-18; Mark 1:21-28).

My First Exorcism

Without any callous intention to crush hopes, it needs to be stated that there is not much value in the power of one's faith *in one's faith*. I, on the other hand, was well aware that this fight belonged to Christ and that a positive outcome was already assured—eventually. I was simply a humble instrument in its achievement. Intellectually I was convinced. But the heart often contradicts the mind. "Is God's Word *really that* efficacious?" I mused, astonished by my own doubts. I was, after all, an ordained minister of God's Church. A higher standard was expected.

Yet from there on, a dreadful downward spiral of disbelief was ignited and with what unmerciful truculence it burned. Scripture passages began popping into my head. But they were all accusatory ones, with the effect of casting doubt upon my ability to carry out my vocational responsibilities. The most troubling was that puzzling text about the disciples unable to cast out some species of demons because they had not prayed or fasted enough, recorded in the seventeenth chapter of St. Matthew's Gospel. I had been praying non-stop. But I had also just had lunch. Was *I* disqualified? I suppose fasting is a method of reminding oneself of one's weaknesses; that Christian piety is not a celebration of one's inherent strength or spiritual achievements, but an unceasing confession that we are simply empty broken vessels which God chooses to use regardless. We are not friendlier, happier or stronger when we are hungry. Fasting exposes our true nature, demonstrating not our capabilities, but our incapabilities. Because *we ate* of the fruit in the Garden, *Jesus fasts* for forty days in the wilderness. He achieves a unique victory by Himself when all of humankind sits in defeat. The solitude and asceticism of fasting does not reveal our virtues. It is not an invitation to look inside of ourselves for spiritual assistance.[4] Rather, it unmasks our sinfulness. Praise God for this, for Christ came not for the righteous, but for sinners. In any case I still regretted eating lunch, for a more practical reason: I felt that it might just make its way up again.

Another unnerving doubt crept into the compromised lucidity of my racing thoughts. I was harassed by the Biblical account of people trying to cast out demons in Jesus' name but failing. The evil spirit retorted with, "Jesus I know, and Paul I recognize, but who are you?" (Acts 19:15) before he pounced on those disciples and beat them up so terribly that they tore out of the house naked and bleeding. What if the same happened to me?

---

4. After all, having us turn inwards upon ourselves—the source of all problems—is the strategy of demons. God commands and invites us to turn outwards towards Him as the single source of hope, peace, joy and salvation.

The Art of Exorcising

Or what about demonic transference—when the demon targets a victim in close proximity to the possessed?[5] This was definitely not what I had signed up for when I consented to become a pastor. Didn't the Holy Spirit and I have some kind of agreement? What about employee rights? Funeral requests from Masonic Lodge members I could handle, wedding requests by fornicating lovers I could deal with, emotionally-charged church council meetings I could survive, but *this*? *This* was totally absurd. Let's be sensible. Maybe I could turn around and refer it to some else. Why hadn't my faithful pastor friend, who assured me that "we are a team," ever called me back? I resented him, blamed him, and even—with a little help from the devil—hated him. I wasn't ready. Is humility still a virtue? Was this even humility or was it pride? There is, after all, a fine line between arrogance and self-confidence. Exorcism can be dangerous and humiliating. For this reason, humility is of paramount importance for exorcists. Saint Teresa explained how, when an exorcist abhors everything about oneself and clings only to the cross, the devil is deprived of all of his weapons. Otherwise, we allow the demons to fight against us with our own tools; handing over to them what we need for our defense.[6] Anyways, besides my lack of piety, the book said that these sorts of matters were supposed to be handled by a bishop or ecclesiastical supervisor. "Perhaps I should turn around and call him right now!" My mind was plagued with all sorts of doubts, subtle forces dissuading me from completing the quest. In a hyperventilating state of panic and speechlessness, the *Jesus Prayer*, mumbled from my failing lips: "Lord, have mercy on me." When we hit rock bottom, tormented by doubt, and have nothing else to offer, the Holy Spirit intercedes. No wonder our prayers sound like His. In fact, in those scattered yet prized moments of life, we realize that we never have *anything* to offer. The best prayers are Scriptures "prayed back" to God, so to speak.

I parked the car. I rang the bell. Debby opened the door without vocalizing a word, her haggard head hanging low, swiftly turning away while knocking over a chair in the process and partially tripping over it on her way back to her place. There she sat, in silence, head down, eyes low, groaning

---

5. For a discussion on how this phenomenon does not usually occur to a Christian, but even when it does, it is worth the risk out of brotherly love and since Christ holds the final victory, see Koch 195. Furthermore, clairvoyance and mediumistic abilities are known to cause a kind of transference such as radiesthetic ability through physical contact. Koch 40.

6. Amorth, *An Exorcist*, 64.

and moaning. Although I kept my eyes open and fixed on her, I prayed inside. I recited hymn stanzas in my heart, such as *Jesus, Priceless Treasure*:

> In Thine arms I rest me;
> Foes who would molest me
> Cannot reach me here.
> Though the earth be shaking,
> Every heart be quaking,
> Jesus calms my fear.
> Lightnings flash
> And thunders crash;
> Yet, though sin and hell assail me,
> Jesus will not fail me.[7]

    I kissed my stole. I placed it around my neck. I hung my crucifix in plain sight of whatever was lurking in that smoky room of blighted hopes. I began timidly, "In the name of the Father, and of the Son and of the Holy Spirit." Ideally a private confession followed by holy absolution precedes the rite. In this case, there was no point. Debby was not all there. This was the devil's jurisdiction, and he knew it. Like a beast before it pounces upon its prey lays still and surreptitious, yet ready and conscientious, the demon did not appear perturbed by my presence. Even though I prayed to be filled with courage in fighting this dragon laying waste to God's vineyard and that *he*, instead of *me*, would be struck with terror, this reprobate beast seemed to burst with a raging glee—without any observable motion. *It* was in control, and did not appear at all alarmed or deterred by me. With a mixture of scornful indignation tempered by a cool appreciation that a Christian was present, the demon appeared unshaken—until I started to speak some more, and with confidence.

    As I professed the Apostles' Creed and spoke the Lord's Prayer, her head was raised a tad, and the moans changed their pitch. After all, the Our Father is the paragon of prayers, and the Creeds are, predominantly, an explanation of the *name* of our Trinitarian Lord. Debby's head began waving from side to side in an apparent effort to avoid the sound of my voice while expressing its disapproval. The tables had turned. I read aloud various texts from the Holy Scriptures concerning Jesus and the apostles casting out demons. The bodily thrusts intensified with more exaggerated jerks of her head. Indiscernible words were lazily offered by a beastly tongue. At first they sounded annoyed. Then, mad. Without warning, a

---

7. TLH 347.

The Art of Exorcising

series of embittered low-pitched voices ejaculated short phrases of anguish such as "No," "Go away," "Shut up," and "Leave me alone." Yet they no longer conveyed a threatening tone. Instead, they were pathetic cries, like a whiney kid in the playground who is irritated that he hadn't gotten his way. An eerily hostile feeling of a contentious and inimical nimbus penetrated the relatively stable ambiance when I finally built up the courage to speak directly to the dreadful thing. Reading from my book I stated sternly: "Depart from Debby, you unclean spirit, and make way for the Holy Spirit, in the name of the Father and of the Son and of the Holy Spirit. Amen." The entity became angry. It was fierce, militant. A glass of juice was whipped at me. I continued with vehemence, "In the name of the Lord Jesus, I command you to leave Debby." For the first time, the boisterous thing looked up at me and stared me straight in the eyes. It was the same empty dark eyes that I had witnessed in the other demoniac, Lisa, 12 years earlier. It was all hate. I preferred to circumvent any further eye contact. In the months that followed, I would dread those rare, but unforgettable glances by those penetrating and bewitching eyes. I emphatically repeated the rebuke in the name of the Holy One. She pushed at me and began throwing arbitrary items across the room, screeching clamorously. This went on for a while.

I became impatient. "Why hadn't the damned thing left?" I asked myself, "Did I forget to tell it where to go?" The Roman Catholic exorcist manuals advised scheduling at least two hours per session, and included prayers and rebukes regarding "lingering" demons. At least I was not the only one. But what if I had made things worse? I was hardly prepared. A "proper" exorcism should be preceded by a period of prayer, confession, and fasting, while the "trained" and "commissioned" exorcist is accompanied by witnesses.[8] Would my ill-preparation screw the whole thing up? I tried to remind myself that I was not adjuring this molester of the human race by my weakness, but by the might of the Holy Spirit. I recited the shorter formula for exorcism, as it was easily memorable: "In the name of Jesus the Christ, I command you to leave." The longer formulas required reading. At this point in the encounter it would have been unwise to lift my eyes off of that woman, even for a split second. I uttered the phrase like a mantra, as calmly as I could, but raising the tone of my voice after each recital. I had read somewhere that by incessant application of the glorious name of Christ the exorcist foments the inflammation of demonic activity and purges the surrounding space of all foreboding evil presence. Finally, I

---

8. *Exorcism: The Findings of a Commission convened by the Bishop of Exeter*, 25.

boldly and assertively placed my poised hands on her head and spoke, "As a servant of Christ and by his authority, I set you free from the devil, in the name of the Father and of the Son and of the Holy Spirit. Amen."

A few passing seconds lingered like hours. Finally, Debby, with a burst of energy, catapulted to her feet and lunged herself at me. The launching entity was easy to dodge since she weighed well over 400 lbs. Thank God that it wasn't like that day in the country of the Gadarenes in which the two demon-possessed men were so fierce, that no one could pass them by (Matt 8:28). The demon attempted, once again, to push me over as it staggered towards the door leading to the hallway. Dodging her a second time, I was able to bar the door with the chain. It seems unadvisable to lock oneself in a tiny room with someone possessed by a devil, but my greater fear was what would become of Debby if her body escaped the building. Some instructional materials for exorcism wisely recommend that "appropriate steps be taken to ensure no unscheduled exit before the ministration is complete."[9] Point 14 of *The Exorcism and Blessing of a Person* urges to have the patient well seated in a deep armchair, and even bound, to prevent self-injury. I must admit that I hadn't thought of the niceties, or even the potential legalities. Suddenly, having been seized by a paroxysm of renewed agitation, an invisible force threw Debby against the exterior wall. Debby then leant towards the ground in a short convulsion. The ferocious demon stared at me malignantly. An eerie squawking followed by low-muttered sobs and incoherent interlocutions protruded from the barely vibrating lips.

Within seconds, it recoiled from me into the corner of the room; its forehead glistened with the dew of agony. Livid, teeth clenched under a corrugated brow, the creature tossed its forehead against the wall and pressed it there as if it was glued to a vanishing target. Pinned there like a toy to a cork panel, it began trembling and shaking. The unclean spirit vibrated intensely but without other motion. It behaved as if it was held in place by a magnet, listless and helpless, as I unceasingly rebuked it. The power of the beast was collapsing under the pressure of the words. I rattled off as many applicable Bible verses as I could. The viper shrivelled in the heat of the Scripture recitations, incapacitated, until I stopped talking. At every tiny break of silence, it seemed to regain its strength. My mouth felt dry; my mind depleted. I felt like a Moses holding up the staff in his battle with the Amalekites, but when his arms drooped down in fatigue, the enemy gained the upper hand. I repeatedly rebuked the enemy, well aware that it was uniquely the power

---

9. *Exorcism* 36.

of God's Word which was taming this beast, and was, frankly, petrified to discover the results if I had stopped speaking altogether.

At last, the break-through arrived. It was not a Hollywood ending: a spinning head textured by milky eyes wailing miserably with a snake tipped hissing tongue. Instead a downtrodden, sad, and even stupefying *lovely* voice was heard, sobbing, "Please, please, let me stay, please, please." The demon may have whimpered "us" in the first person plural. I don't remember. It really makes no difference. Like the Queen of Charn in C.S. Lewis' *The Magician's Nephew* the demon(s) were appealing for mercy. Professional exorcists have often witnessed pitiful sighs and pleadings for mercy from demons claiming to be the abused victims.[10] After all, the Word of God is sheer pain for them—hotter than the fire of hell—which is why they eventually depart.[11] But they are also liars, and cannot be trusted. Demons are usually reluctant to speak, except to trick, distract, and threaten. However, when commanded to speak their name in the name of the crucified saviour, they must respond truthfully.[12] Verbalizing their real name is a sign of submission and, hence, defeat.[13] Accordingly, the *Roman Ritual* permits conversation only for interrogation purposes, in order to confirm their presence, determine the number of inhabiting spirits, establish their sources, and decipher details surrounding the circumstances of their entrance or the whereabouts of occult objects that may be hidden in the room, such as in pillows.[14] Experiments, mocking, and too much poking around is dangerous. Clearly, communicating with creatures that are renowned liars and seek our doom is inadvisable. That being said, I was expecting some hostile curses, not this harmless snivel. The whole scene could have been summarized with one word: "pathetic"—in accordance with its truest meaning.

The ordeal represented another one of those surreal moments in my life that I will never forget, chiefly because my reaction was so unexpected: I felt sorry for it! I felt compassion for the evil creature. Despite the fact that he and his company were the perpetrators of all of the world's misery and suffering since the beginning of time, I felt sympathy. I was speechless.

---

10. Vogl 19.

11. Amorth, *An Exorcist*, 115.

12. Ibid.

13 The power of a name should never be underestimated. It is more than simply a pragmatic means of identity. Perhaps the obscure mythological character Rumpelstiltskin has something to teach us about demonology!

14. Amorth, *An Exorcist*, 79.

My First Exorcism

Believe it or not, I was oddly persuaded to ask for its forgiveness! It seems unbelievable today, but at that moment, I wanted to hold its hand and say, "there, there, everything will be okay." As though it were a beaten and bruised puppy, I longed to offer it some water. We clergy are, after all, in the business of showing mercy. Didn't Jesus have compassion on the demons when they begged him to release them into the pigs? "Don't trust your senses Harold," I reminded myself. The devil was the most beautiful of angels, who continues to disguise himself likewise. Certainly this demon was manipulating me, as they are all so accustomed to doing, and using his "good looks" to his own advantage. But he *seemed* so genuine, sincere and honest. "The poor little demon ostracized for being true to himself," I pondered, "just trying to fulfill his dreams like every other disillusioned individual; a misguided soul searching for existential meaning in his dissident existence. It's not his fault that he is an angel trapped in a woman's body. After all, God made Him that way, didn't He? He had no choice, right? And now he suffers from dissociative identity disorder all because of a draconian and ethnocentric supreme being who has little tolerance for difference. No one understands. But I do. Perhaps *he* is not the enemy. Maybe *God* is!" For a moment I believed that however vicious it may have once been, this demon was, deep down, *good*. And conceivably they were all like that. For one instantaneous moment—a brief second—I even wondered *if I was on the right side*! Were the *Rolling Stones* correct; does the devil warrant our sympathy?

My gut advised me to comfort it. My feelings nudged me to give it a hug. Its agony unrelentingly increased. I continued to suffer a crisis of conscience and genuine guilt. "Maybe I could find it a new home or, at the very least, let it stay, just for a little while longer. Canadians are supposed to be polite, aren't we?" The suggestion acted as a mentally and spiritually soothing and picturesque oasis in the midst of this sadistic and desiccated desert. Meanwhile, Debby's weakened body yielding a strained whimpering voice, leaned against the wall in desperate defeat. The motion startled something inside of this deadly stream of consciousness probing me to whisper to myself, "Snap out of it Harold!" What on earth was I thinking? Repent.

+ + +

Why was I so remarkably tempted to engage in conversation with this antichristian villain for whom I felt such irrational compassion? Maybe it was because of all that the evil one and I held together in common: we were old friends after all, or even brothers, in that other life, before my gracious Lord paid the ransom and rescued me through the sacrament of Holy Baptism. But even as the Old Adam remains, an affiliation stays intact. The devilish damage had already been done, an acquaintance with evil cultivated from humankind's very first conversation with the devil. The old self may even resent this merciful and divine kidnapping by Christ. After all, it did occur without our permission, an infringement of inherent human rights. Our primordial reasoning remains set by unholy dimensions. The insult ought not to surprise us. Humans are, after all, living-dead creatures. Our sinful bodies are half alive, yet still not half of what God anticipated for us. We are walking corpses; partially alive, but residing in a perpetual state of dying.[15] From the moment of our birth we reluctantly but persistently make our way towards the grave. In this state, hell is our true home. We can boast of no dimension of our human existence untainted by sin. As the Church sings along with German poet and pastor, Johann Heermann, "There was no spot in me by sin untainted; sick with sin's inflicted poison, all my heart had fainted; my heavy guilt to hell had well-nigh brought me, such woe it wrought me."[16] The flames, smells, and sights of sin are not unfamiliar to the deepest chambers of our souls. We sense this when we are sick, unhappy, unfulfilled, deprived of peace, worried, and, in short, lacking rest. Something is not right. Yet we still have hope. Like a crazed addict, high on cocaine, who still knows, deep down, that this is not his true self—there is a cure. We have an antidote. Death has been reconstructed as the doorway to life. Our final enemy reluctantly serves as the valet into the kingdom of God. There is no longer any need to fear. Death has been swallowed up in victory. Through our Lord's death we have been offered the way to life. The dead now only sleep. The living are no longer condemned. The accusations that belong to us have been absorbed into the precious body of Jesus and in Him crucified.

The timeless question "Why do bad things happen to good people?" is prompted by an egocentric self-understanding. "Why do *good* things happen to *bad* people?" of whom each of us is chief (1 Tim 1:15), is a more appropriate question. The goading confession in the *Compline*, "I have sinned in thought, word and deed by *my* fault, by *my own* fault, by *my own most*

---

15. This is especially applicable to the unconverted as St. Paul calls them *nekrous* or the "walking dead" (Eph 2:1). Bennett 157.

16. LSB 439.

grievous fault"[17] contains injurious words indeed. They expose our impure hearts. They thwart all inquiries into theodicy and other covetous hunger for forbidden fruits of knowledge that are not ours to possess. When we believe ourselves to be entitled to the answer to our questions, our omnipotent Creator rebukes us with, "Where were you when I laid the foundation of the earth? Tell me, if you have understanding" (Job 38:4). God owes us nothing, while we owe Him everything. Instead we receive in life from the bountiful goodness of God, not what we deserve—thanks be to Him—but what we do *not* deserve. "Though the heart is a rusty old can on a junk heap," as Swedish bishop Bo Giertz writes, "a wonderful Lord passes by, and has mercy on the wretched tin can, sticks His walking cane through it and rescues it from the junk pile and takes it home with him."[18] Now, released from a well-warranted curse, we *have* been set free. The load has been lifted off of our backs and placed upon Him. And He who has raised Himself can certainly raise others: "Since therefore the children share in flesh and blood, he himself likewise partook of the same things, that through death he might destroy the one who has the power of death, that is, the devil" (Heb 2:14). We deserve nothing from life and yet we graciously receive all the treasures of heaven and loads of temporal benefits as well. Life would truly be a living hell if God did not intervene at every moment throughout the day.

Although His human enemies—those who have consciously or unconsciously rejected His means of salvation and grace—have already begun to breathe hell's fumes (John 3:18), God refuses to let them slip away without a fight. Even delaying His return has truly shown "the immeasurable riches of his grace in kindness toward us in Christ Jesus" (Eph 2:7). Forgive the cliché, but instead of complaining about the things that we do not possess, we ought to be thankful for those things that we do. And when we honestly feel ourselves to be short-changed despite all praiseworthy arguments from reason, our Good Shepherd patiently forgives and still reigns supreme. Crushed hopes are illusions that have no grounding in reality, for "Jesus lives! the vict'ry's won."[19]

Most people want a bargain. But when it comes to the heavenly kingdom, we are easily distracted from God's overall beauty by *perceived*

---

17. LSB 254.

18. Giertz, *The Hammer of God*, 147. After all, one man's trash is another man's treasure! Thanks be to God.

19. LSB 490.

blemishes. One could compare this spiritual reluctance to embrace true religion to a consumer's hesitation to buy a pristine car at a bargain price because of a scratch detected on the polish of the back bumper, only to discover later on that there was no scrape on the vehicle—but there was one across the lens of the customer's eyeglasses! Yet even with the scratch, however unreal, the skeptic makes a stupid choice. The veracity of Christian truth-claims remains in spite of our lack of believing them at any particular moment of our lives. The devil deludes. We are habitually duped by misguided perceptions. My lapse in faith and twisted reasoning was evident in the perverse yearning to befriend this pathetic beast through Debby, its channel. Gollum from Tolkein's *The Hobbit* offers a rough comparison. One fears him at first, and then pities him thereafter. But it is a trap. He is untrustworthy and dangerous.

Due to my curiosity and compassion for the demon, I had gradually and unintentionally lost interest in the welfare of Debby. I had unknowingly objectified this anguishing child in my personal pursuit of self-improvement under an imagined guise of "professional development." Even after my repentant plea (sigh) I was still tempted to converse with the demon some more, retracing its origins, interests, hobbies, etc. Like a zoologist analyzing a newly discovered species on the Galapagos Islands, I had cornered and caged this fascinating species. What an opportunity! Debby had become for me a utilitarian tool for an unholy end. I suppose there are no selfless acts. The Psalmist writes, "There is none who does good, not even one" (Ps 53:3). All of us subconsciously misuse others, but this endeavour was so obvious it was embarrassing. The intellectual in me was pertinaciously curious. As a doctor of Religious Studies, I was highly interested in the scientific process, with an inquisitiveness that demanded pacification. I would press on in research to my tenacious satisfaction...but wait. No. What was happening to me? It was I who was imprisoned. I was the one being toyed with and played by this callous raider on its last cruel foray. "Have mercy on me, O God, according to your steadfast love; according to your abundant mercy blot out my transgressions. Wash me thoroughly from my iniquity, and cleanse me from my sin!" (Ps 51:1–2) I prayed. "Depart from me, you unclean spirit! I am baptized, and you cannot have me!" is what I thought. Yet, "Shut up! Be quiet!" is what I cried out.

My First Exorcism

+ + +

It is always a bad idea to dialogue with demons. They are smarter and more powerful than us, especially when we vulnerable sheep decide to wander away from the bulwark of the sheepfold, distancing ourselves from the Good Shepherd. Jesus would always silence demons, without exception. He shuts the mouths of lions. Even on the rare occasions that the demons confessed the truth, albeit mockingly addressing Him as "Son of the Most High," Jesus ordered them to be quiet and did not permit them to speak further (Mark 1:34). When they asked to be sent into the herd of swine, He simply said, "go"—and they went. The Word of God is a powerful tool in creation. After all, the Word which formed all things visible and invisible became flesh and dwells among us. Hence, the *lying word* is equally dangerous. The worst is always an abuse of the best. But I had the Word of Christ! I possessed the keys of the kingdom: the ability to loose and to bind (Matt 16:19)! And here I was binding. This divine ability belongs to the pastoral office, a duty better known as "excommunication." Of course, excommunication is intended to drive an unrepentant sinner back to the shelter and shade of the cross of Christ's forgiveness. This does not apply to demons. They have eternally excommunicated themselves from the kingdom of God. Yet most people do the same when they disregard church in general, or the reception of Holy Communion (i.e. "ex-communion"), in particular. But church discipline still exists. The last time I had used those binding keys publicly were at a Christmas Eve service through an ancient rite where the General Absolution "In the stead and by the command of my Lord Jesus Christ, I forgive you all your sins in the name of the Father, and of the Son and of the Holy Spirit" continues with "For those unrepentant of their sins, by the same command and authority, I bind your sins in the name of the...."[20] For clergy that want to exorcize the "holiday spirit" and eradicate all other forms of sentimentalism from "warm and fuzzy" Christmas Eve celebrations, here is a tool at their disposal. In fact, I managed to cut attendance in half the following year! Without wilfully resonating the puritanism of a Donatist form of heresy, one that seeks to separate the

---

20. The full declaration reads: "On the other hand, by the same authority, I declare unto the impenitent and unbelieving, that so long as they continue in their impenitence, God hath not forgiven their sins, and will assuredly visit their iniquities upon them, if they turn not from their evil ways, and come to true repentance and faith in Christ, ere the day of grace be ended." From the rite of Public Confession in *The Service Book and Hymnal* 252.

visible Church from the invisible Church before the final harvest—as I do believe that it is usually better for people to attend church, even when their intentions are questionable—it is too bad that there are no plaques awarded for "church pruning" as there are for "church growth." True church growth is not contingent upon numbers. One must retain a sense of humour in keeping the priorities of eternity in perspective. But in all seriousness, here I stood, binding this demon, from both Debby and myself, with the Lord's strong word cleaving the darkness through my broken, yet, evidently, efficacious, lips.

It left. She tumbled to the ground, relieved, at ease. Praise God.

> Satan, I defy thee;
> Death, I now decry thee;
> Fear, I bid thee cease.
> World, thou shalt not harm me
> Nor thy threats alarm me
> While I sing of peace.
> God's great power Guards every hour;
> Earth and all its depths adore Him,
> Silent bow before Him.[21]

---

21. TLH 347.

Who's Afraid of the Steppenwolf?

> And they came to Jesus and saw the demon-possessed man, the one who had had the legion, sitting there, clothed and in his right mind, and they were afraid. (Mark 5:15)

And that was how my first exorcism ended. Arguably, it is a bit anti-climactic. A noticeable relaxation replaced the formerly tense spiritual environment. Debby stumbled to the toilet and started vomiting uncontrollably. In our later episodes together, I noted that whenever a demon was released, she would repeat this behaviour in the bathroom, even if they were only dry heaves. It seemed to indicate that the demons had fled, or had been transferred—maybe in the absence of a pig farm the drainpipe to a sewage treatment plant did the trick. Since then, I have learned that vomiting frequently follows an exorcism. In fact, in cases where witchcraft is the cause, items such as glass, nails, knotted strings, rolled wires, and even small wooden dolls are vomited out, even when these objects were not necessarily swallowed previously. Although the notion of teleportation may have its origins in the sphere of science fiction and *Star Trek*, the idea may not be as far-fetched as it first sounds. St. Paul knew a man who "was caught up into paradise—whether in the body or out of the body I do not know, God knows—and he heard things that cannot be told, which man may not utter" (2 Cor 12:3–4). Incidentally, this passage is written within the context of spiritual and demonic warfare. In any case, exorcists are advised to burn all such cursed objects that have been extracted from a demoniac, while praying over them—never touching them—and scattering the ashes over running water.[1] Although I myself would not advocate it, the consumption of holy water is also, allegedly, a great help in patient recovery.[2]

The intricate union between the body and soul is undeniable. It is typified in such *physical* repercussions of *spiritual* battle—how spiritual phenomena impact physical elements. The Apocryphal book of *Ecclesiasticus* observes how wickedness has the potential to change one's physical appearance (Sir 25:17). Positively speaking, God has always remained tangibly present with His people: from the Ark of the Covenant in the days of old, to His means of grace today. Negatively, evil also boasts its tangible manifestations. In one recorded case of demon possession in 1928, the demoniac clung to the wall like a spider, while the nuns had difficulty bringing her back to the mattress.[3] The poor Iowa girl was cursed by her despicable and unchaste father who offered her to the devil after she refused to commit incest with him. She, as well, vomited buckets of strange substances daily, even though she had barely eaten anything during the twenty-three day exorcism.[4] In addition, some stomach fluids were habitually spat from the girl whose body had become so discoloured and disfigured through unusual bloating that its regular contours were unrecognizable. The peculiar fluctuation of the bodily weight even resulted in the permanent bending of the metal bed-frame.[5]

Other exorcists record the manifestation of burn marks and bruising on the patient, the smell of sulphuric odours, the presence of multiple voices, unusual behaviour from house pets, and a vast unimaginable range of other frightening manifestations.[6] Supernatural occurrences accompanying demon possession are not uncommon, which is why the Roman Ritual of 1618 includes the following clues as confirmation of the diagno-

1. Amorth, *More Stories*, 156.

2. Amorth, *An Exorcist*, 118. Incidentally, the massive volume of UFO sightings cannot simply be dismissed as delusions, hoaxes or hallucinations. Yet if God created life on other planets those creatures would also have suffered the consequences of the Fall. It is as probable, however, that these sightings have demonic origins. Some Christians have hypothesized that aliens are embodied demons. Strong apparitions of evil spirits have been known to scratch people with fingers and hold them with hands. Can claims of extra-terrestrial abductions be explained by demonic embodiment? It sounds absurd, but if some have entertained angels unaware (Heb 13:2), perhaps the same principle applies to the fallen angels as well.

3. Vogl 13.

4. Ibid 19.

5. Vogl 21.

6. Amorth, *An Exorcist*, 124.

sis: the ability to communicate with some facility in a strange or foreign tongue (such as Latin); the faculty to divulge future and hidden events; and the capacity to display powers that are beyond the subject's age and natural condition.[7] Seventeenth-century Lutheran theologian Johannes Andreas Quenstedt also listed monstrosity in gestures, obscenity in speech, clairvoyance, self-hatred, and the capability to voice exact reproductions of animal noises without the disposition of the required organs.[8] If there is indeed a connection between physical health and spirituality, it ought to come of no surprise that at the Lord's casting out of demons the mute speak and the deaf hear (Matt 9:32–33). The association is clear in collects of the Church such as the following:

> Lord Jesus, Holy One of God, You showed that the kingdom of God had come by Your healing the sick and casting out demons. Heal us in both body and soul by the medicine of Your body and blood that we may truly be your disciples. Amen.[9]

Demon possession is a compelling argument against Gnostic beliefs in the bifurcation of body and soul. Our neo-Gnostic world today is buttressed by such philosophically-driven demarcations. Most people live as if the body and soul have nothing in common with one another. In contrast, the Hebrew definition of man or *ish* is something like "embodied soul." Yet one often hears from well-meaning Christians that the body is simply a cage for the soul, denying any real sacred union between the two. Accordingly, many Christians have difficulty believing in the efficaciousness of the sacraments. How can natural water, bread and wine distribute spiritual goods? The popularity of Eastern spirituality, mysticism and meditation represent efforts at escaping the physical world.

We can, however, learn a few things from other religions. The attention that Muslims give to posture in prayer is one of them. Prayer is not treated simply an intellectual exercise, but a whole body-soul experience. In C.S. Lewis's *The Screwtape Letters*, the fictional demon, Screwtape, indicates to his colleague, Wormwood, that humans, who have forgotten their creaturely status,

> can be persuaded that the bodily position makes no difference to their prayers; for they constantly forget, what you must always

---

7. *The Roman Ritual*, 217.
8. Bennett 150.
9. *Treasury of Daily Prayer*, 29.

remember, that they are animals and that whatever their bodies do affects their souls.[10]

Muslims bow, kneel and prostrate themselves in accordance with the ancient Judeo-Christian way. Very few Christians still kneel when they pray. We isolate our minds from external acts of piety. By keeping their Koran high off of the floor, it would seem as if Muslims respect the written word more than we do. We prefer to dismiss their reverence as superstition lest it necessitate that we reassess our own lack of respect. Although God *buried* Moses (Deut 34:6) neo-Gnostic tendencies explain the rapidly increasing popularity of cremation over burial in Western Christian churches.[11] The fact that churches today have, for the most part, incorporated these anti-Christian beliefs into their own worldviews is betrayed by the overwhelming disinterest in discussing the subject and the disparaging attitude by faithful believers who snub the proposition that these practices should still be prone to serious questioning in the twenty-first century. Historical obliviousness amongst laity and clergy alike does not help the cause. Yet burial confesses the sanctity of all created elements. All things are good despite the corruption by sin, evil and death. It confesses a heaven that is both a spiritual and a physical place: a new heaven and *a new earth* (Rev 21:1). St. Paul presumes these misconceptions in his sermons to the Church in Corinth that had difficulty believing in a physical resurrection due to a docetic belief in a chasm between things spiritual and physical. He describes the sort of new creatures that we will one day become as not bodiless angels, but redeemed and beautified *creatures*: "For this perishable body must put on the imperishable, and this mortal body must put on immortality" (1 Cor 15:54). The ways that we treat our bodies betray our bias. So too, Christians ought to be less exigent in their questionings of parapsychology and paranormal activities than their unbelieving neighbours.

---

10. Lewis, *The Screwtape Letters*, 11.

11. During waves of persecution, like today in many countries of the world, churches are often burned down to the ground, and with people inside of them. So, too, the holy martyrs were burned at the stake. Although they all enter heaven (and participate in the resurrection of the dead with newly glorified bodies) such disposal of their physical bodies was never by choice. In the case where ashes are unavoidable, their scattering is. As Johann Heermann wrote in O *God, My Faithful God*: "Let me depart this life confiding in my Savior; By grace receive my soul that it may live forever; And let my body have a quiet resting place *within a Christian grave*; And let it sleep in peace" (LSB 696). Belief in the physical resurrection of the dead does everything within its power to respectfully and reverently prepare the cadaver (or its remains) for that glorious and happy day.

My First Exorcism

Incidentally, Gnosticism is a distant cousin of rationalism, empiricism and all other offspring of the Enlightenment.

In short, I am convinced that Debby's vomiting was not simply a natural physical side-effect of a traumatic experience. Furthermore, for me, it functioned as a sign that the exorcism had reached a successful result. I even began to watch for it. For the demons returned, more than once, and all too often. I cannot even recollect the number of visits that I had made to that gloomy apartment in the months that followed. Yet the worst memory is the haunting ease with which my heart filled with compassion when hearing the desperate and seemingly sincere voice of that demon appealing to my compassion. Heartlessly depraved, but frightfully convincing. Positively, I have gained a new perspective on the temptation of Jesus in the desert, as the devil appealed to *His* sense of compassion as well: "Turn the stones to bread and you can feed the world and solve global hunger; take the kingdom of the earth and you can rule as the most just and fair judge for all time—but whatever you do, *do not go to the cross!*" St. Peter suggests a similar request of his Lord (Matt 16:22). In both cases Jesus' love for His father and all humankind compelled Him to respond with "Be gone Satan" and "Get behind me Satan." Waging war with the prince of this earth remains a cross that Christ's body continues to drag through the beaten alleys and bloodied streets of the Christian life. If Jesus was susceptible to temptation, His followers will enjoy no exemption. "Resist him, firm in your faith, knowing that the same kinds of suffering are being experienced by your brotherhood throughout the world" (1 Peter 5:9). Yet Christ stands amidst His brothers in every one of their fiery furnaces. And the same weapons harnessed by our Lord to extinguish these blazing darts—the faithful proclamation uttered in the words "It is written"—remain our sword, whilst the Creed, our shield.

+ + +

The Christian struggle is occasionally interrupted with moments of jubilation. When I left Debby's place, I was on an emotional and spiritual "high." The whole afternoon was an adrenaline rush, I bashfully admit. Like an athlete flaunting a newly gained prize, I felt on top of the world. As seventy-two joyful disciples conveyed to the Lord, "Even the demons are subject to us in your name!" (Luke 10:17), I now shared in that satisfying sensation. Astonished at the majesty of God, I too was utterly amazed at

Who's Afraid of the Steppenwolf?

the power of God's Word in achieving its goals. I had always believed, but now I saw. As doubting Thomas was told, "Have you believed because you have seen me? Blessed are those who have not seen and yet have believed" (John 20:29). Only the weak in faith require a miracle. I am not ashamed to admit that I fall under that category. But still, such a glimpse into His might is an uncommon occurrence; an invitation to place one's hand into the side of the Lord is not to be shunned. Miracles are gifts, not rewards. Still Jesus warns that He has given "authority to tread on serpents and scorpions, and over all the power of the enemy, and nothing shall hurt you. Nevertheless, do not rejoice in this, that the spirits are subject to you, but rejoice that your names are written in heaven" (Luke 10:19–20) since much of life can be characterized by suffering. The greatest miracles are unseen.

Meanwhile, what ascends descends. This one plummeted with a crash. The giddy excitement quickly spiralled down into utter exhaustion. I just wanted to sleep. That day I felt as I would years later, when as a military chaplain and parachutist, I would tumble out of airplanes using out-dated WWII training equipment: while beginning on a high, hitting the ground hurts. The impact is severe. Every bone ached and every nerve shook. But despite the pain, it was worth it.

+ + +

Although escorting this new catechumen through a lengthy program of instruction was my original plan, Debby was baptized the following Sunday. *This* was an emergency. I won't lie; it took some convincing to get her baptized. This is not to say that she was not happy with "her decision," but she did not find it intuitive. After all, Holy Baptism divorces us from the devil and marries us to Christ. It is life-altering and should never be entered into lightly. It is a nuptial union reserved not only for celibate priests or nuns. It is the most important day in every believer's life. The baptismal rite is then followed by a wedding feast, or at least a culinary nibble of the "foretaste of the feast to come" as is spoken in one preface for Holy Communion. For that meal, however, Debby would need to wait a while. Not yet authorized to eat, she was still seated at the table in the only home in which any of us finally belong. Following Christ becomes an aimless wandering when at the end of the week we fail to follow Jesus into His home.

I also enquired into whether or not Debby would permit me to bless her home. House blessings are advisable for all Christians. Whenever I move residence, I execute the extraordinary liturgy of house blessing, taking advantage of the same service offered to parishioners. The practice is not superstitious, but a wholesome expression of a living faith that seeks to claim unfamiliar space for God. It is a kind of spiritual house cleaning, consecrating homes as sanctuaries undefiled. My family has adopted the practice of praying the Litany on Wednesday evenings as a means of re-consecrating the area from any secluded evil influences. Things used in church are consecrated in order to free them from the domination of evil. Our home life is an extension of weekly worship. Places can be stained by evil incurred by others. While some hire Shamans to burn sage or they practice yoga in an effort to rid any "negative energy" from a dwelling place, Christians ask for pastors, priests and exorcists. Yet the hangovers of evil deeds aren't always manifested in hauntings, poltergeists, or psychic activities. A house may have been a site of questionable moral activity. In every case, we offer the space back to Christ. Interestingly, in Shintoism the Japanese ritually clean their houses as an effort of *inviting* the spirits of the dead inside. We Christians ask them to leave. We use collects such as "Visit our dwellings, O Lord, and drive from them all the snares of the enemy; let Your holy angels dwell with us to preserve us in peace; and let Your blessing be on us always."[12] Conceivably, a room of the house could have been consecrated to ungodly forces by prior owners. Sometimes houses are hexed due to previous use as a location for séances, organized crime, and abnormal sexual activity. Evil disorders can affect objects, animals and places.[13] Yet Satanists do not hold a monopoly on desecration. Average sinners may invite demons unaware. At the very least, a house blessing is a symbolic gesture announcing that the home will be used in holy ways, offered to God by a holy people. In cases of suspicious paranormal activity, even cupboard doors may be opened with prayers recited such as,

> Deliver this place from all evil spirits; all vain imaginations, projections and phantasms, and all deceits of the evil one; and bid them harm no one but depart to the place appointed them, there to remain forever.[14]

Many Christians place crosses and crucifixes in their homes or fix Bible verses to walls in accordance with the same reasoning. Sometimes salt and

---

12. LSB 257.
13. Amorth, *More Stories*, 156.
14. *Exorcism* 32.

holy water are used to symbolize the re-hallowing of space and objects for use by the baptized.[15] A house blessing also offers the chance to pray, several times, once in each room. Families should pray together. Pastors should visit them. There is no harm in any of that. Traditionally a cross for the wall was offered as a gift by the visiting clergyman. Apparently the wooden ones work best. There are accounts of demoniacs mocking some crucifixes that were less of a resemblance of the true Christ, such as one made out of paper mache. With a sneering and ridiculing laughter, one demon jeered, "Ha, so you arrived with a pasteboard cross! Since when did 'He' die on a paper cross?"[16] St. Cyril of Jerusalem calls every cross and crucifix the "dread of devils."[17] Sometimes things matter. After an exorcism, the disposal of satanic books and occult items is in order, but so is the re-dedication of the space. Unfortunately however, all these religious acts did not fix the problem for Debby. Just as alcoholics have relapses, and as each of us cave into the various idiosyncratic temptations of our own lives, so did Debby. Consequently, the demons returned with a vengeance. Well-intentioned, she longed to surrender herself entirely to Jesus. The New Testament promises, "Submit yourselves therefore to God. Resist the devil, and he will flee from you" (Jas 4:7). But it also says that, "The spirit is willing but the flesh is weak" (Mark 14:38). We all make mistakes. We are dogs that return to our vomit in some manner or another. And, certainly, we are never cast away but instead we are forgiven, for "If we are faithless, he will remain faithful . . . for he cannot deny himself" (2 Tim 2:13). But we still live with the ravages of our sins. And each sin generates a vast array of dismal repercussions.

---

15. Objects and figurines of heathen and occult worship can be "crystallization points" of demonic power. Koch 92. Most hand-carved artifacts such as masks and other exotic souvenirs fail to include their history or record of their prior usage. Yet Christians should not become excessively afraid of the possibility of haunted or occult objects in their house. The grace and power of Holy Baptism extends over all of our ignorance as well. However, "Everyone to whom much was given, of him much will be required, and from him to whom they entrusted much, they will demand the more" (Luke 12:48). Once we "know better" we are expected to act boldly and faithfully (2 Peter 2:21). Furthermore, the New Testament logic of handling food dedicated to idols seems to apply to all objects reserved for evil purposes (1 Cor 8:1–13). Nothing is intrinsically evil since all things were created good by the heavenly Creator. Instead things become bad in their ungodly use.

16. Vogl 25.

17. St. Cyril of Jerusalem, *Catechetical Lecture*, 13.36.

My First Exorcism

+ + +

For the next six weeks, there were severe struggles as Debby relapsed to her old ways and the demons returned with augmented virulence. She would regularly and consistently call me to rescue her. From a mental health and pastoral counselling perspective, it was far from perfect. Sometimes her relapses involved cocaine usage, other hallucinogenic drugs, and sexual defilement coupled with occult games and rituals. It was not uncommon for her to confess episodes of bodily levitation. At first, she despondently hid the fact that she had conserved certain occult paraphernalia, even after her conversion to Christ and her baptism. Sometimes she would reject me with scoff. The demons are clever. They know how to hide. I would test Debby to see if they were gone by insisting that she speak the holy name of our Lord or recite a Scripture verse. Even those who are only demonically oppressed are often unable to speak the holy name. However reminiscent of a *Harry Potter* story, in which the protagonists are forbidden to utter the unholy name of "Voldemort" due to its inherent magical power, the supernatural power contained in the name of Jesus protruding from a believer's lips is neither fable nor joke. One demonically-subjected individual who wrote to a Christian counsellor could only say, "the one who hangs on the cross...you know who I mean."[18] So when Debby resisted or was unable to speak the name of Jesus Christ, I knew that the demons had returned. And it didn't take long before they unveiled their ugly faces. What I didn't know then was that this was all "normal."[19] Complete liberation could sometimes take years, and in rare cases, full deliverance occurred only after death![20] "The way to healing is sincere conversion"[21] observed one catholic exorcist, and complete deliverance requires the willingness and cooperation of the one possessed; openness to the ministry of the Gospel coupled with a repentant attitude. Even Jesus couldn't/wouldn't perform miracles in faithless places (Matt 13:58). Even so, I pressed on, bitterly at times, overcoming many paroxysms of impatience and exasperation. And each irritating exorcism took more time. So Jesus had likewise warned,

> When the unclean spirit has gone out of a person, it passes through waterless places seeking rest, and finding none it says, 'I will return

---

18. Koch 141–142.
19. Vogl 47.
20. Amorth, *An Exorcist*, 73.
21. Ibid 59.

to my house from which I came.' And when it comes, it finds the house swept and put in order. Then it goes and brings seven other spirits more evil than itself, and they enter and dwell there. And the last state of that person is worse than the first (Luke 11:24–26).

I was determined to continue fighting, even if I believed that I would eventually lose. One is accountable to God who is the ultimate judge. There was a time when people fought for principles in spite of foreseeable and incontestable defeat. Today utilitarianism overrides determinations to martyrdom. Kamikazes had misplaced goals, but they were willing to die for something greater than their own personal interests—namely, family honour. People once believed that there were worse things than death. The modernizing societies of the Western world are replacing a traditional Christian worldview with a secularist one that declares values antithetical to those of its forefathers. Most people no longer attend public worship. But they still thrive on the idea of churches, cherish Christian art, and are intrigued by ecclesiastical architecture. Our present generation appears semi-willing to swallow the religious sediment of a Bach cantata as a small price to pay in digesting its aesthetic quality. This sentimentalism divulges an indulgent, extravagant and superfluous generation that relishes archaic cultural icons for decoration's sake. What it fails to realize is that this Christian furniture cannot be restricted to an ideological museum but is a heritage permanently embedded on a moral floor that still provides the ground for the anatomical structure of Western society. When that nexus is withdrawn, a bottomless hole remains. What the "progressive" liberal-minded carelessly neglect to appreciate is that stripping society of these Christian artifacts leaves a vacuum that they are not able to fill. Even many of the early postmodern subjectivists and deconstructionists insinuate that the Christian suppositions underlying secular society were, ultimately, its sole saving grace.[22]

The baby boomers criticize "organized" religion though their "disorganized" versions are laughable substitutes. I suppose that the second law of thermodynamics may also apply to the supposed evolution of religion. The Hippies of the Sixties continue—however unknowingly—to actively convey many idiomatic Christian values to their children such as showing

22. Although they did not believe that the foundation underlying the philosophical presuppositions of any culture could be entirely known, they underscored the danger involved when believing that that foundation did not exist at all: "The future carries the burden of all our pasts. That's why it's important to know of how many forgotten words it is made." Edmond Jabès, *From the Desert to the Book: Dialogues with Marcel Cohen*, 45.

respect to others, treating people equally, displaying an indiscriminate justice, loving one's neighbour as oneself, etc.—all of which are concretized in our Western charters and underpin her constitutions.[23] The trouble is that these documents are living entities that can be amended, and only have force when they are believed. For example, the dregs of a Christian society are still evident in a common belief that citizens should, through government institutions, care for each other. The Geneva Conventions owe their presuppositions to Christian chivalry and etiquette. During WWII Western nations committed war crimes, but they denied them. Today, ISIS extols them. The communists and many Asian armies never held themselves accountable to the sort of ethical values reflected in those of the West. In the Middle East, the Taliban shot at NATO troops from Minarets. In general, we deem it unthinkable to destroy a religious site, even when it may mean forfeiting a victory. The feelings are not mutual. Many of our values are hangovers from past generations. But a rupture has occurred. Times have changed, and "Wisdom is justified by all her children" (Luke 7:35). In North America, Europe and Australia a new and "twisted generation" (Matt 17:17) is arising that will have inherited none of these presuppositions from its parents. If we actually lived by the Social Darwinian slogan, "Look out for number one; survival of the fittest," our society would collapse. Communities founded on that principle will quickly surrender to invading forces, whether economic or political. Clearly, many non-Western nations still believe that there are things worth fighting for beyond individual self-interest and the prosaic god of materialism. Their gusto overrides our own. At least we still have conscience, but even that can mislead us at times. Thank God for Christians who pray—for everybody else.

+ + +

Prayer always helps. It was my only help in my half-baked mental state. Spiritually and emotionally fatigued, how frustrated had I become

---

23. Recently the Supreme Court of Canada ruled against permitting prayers in public spaces. Freedom *of* religion is now understood to include freedom *from* religion where unbelief is held as a legitimate form of belief, and with the result that the god of atheism becomes the one subtly invoked in the pretend neutral public space. In short, in spite of the claims of popular postmodernism and their homage paid to subjectivity, neutrality is a rare state as every vacuum begs to be filled with something. It is remarkable, however, that a governmental agency would implicitly admit to the favouritism of one religion over the next (i.e. the religion of secularism) in such a transparent manner.

with these recurrent discouraging visits to that dreadful apartment. At every junction, it felt as though Debby, whose depressions were now more acute, would counteract my arduous labour through her dispassionate backslidings and melancholy attitudes. I had even grown accustomed to the unholy clamour, finding it predictable, but had yet to become numb to the demonic possessions overall. I was tired—and spooked. I knew that it was common for the devil to work in the heart of exorcists out of vengeance or in order to dissuade them from returning. When Martin Luther hurled an ink bottle at an apparition, he was not alone. Even though hauntings and physical attacks are easily addressed by short formulas for exorcizing evil spirits, I wasn't in the mood to investigate. Instead, my greatest comfort was secured in the fact that the life of Jesus Christ is typological of the pastoral ministry. While He is the suffering Servant, pastors are microcosmic versions. The chief Shepherd is the ultimate carrier of all of our burdens. Yet we clergy also bear our share of the consequences of other people's spiritual baggage and emotional loads, "patiently enduring evil" (2 Tim 2:24) out of love for Him.

This motif struck home while serving in Afghanistan. I was a stupendously proud witness of soldiers who exist, truly, as suffering servants. Though often foul-mouthed and lacking in tactfulness, they were each one, singularly, heroes. Soldiers carry out a holy vocation by reason of its sheer legality. Although these specially commissioned agents take no pleasure in killing, they function as God's divine tools in providing national security. This unique legalized application of violence is a necessary evil; a dirty job that some consecrated victims must perform on behalf of the rest of us. While praying for peace we thank God for warriors.[24] Members of the military represent all the citizens of their respective countries in war. But they alone suffer the ramifications: personal guilt, family friction, physical wounds and mental injury. Although we pray in the *Litany* "against a sudden and evil death" the odds are fixed against some.

The infantry haul the repercussions of our sin—just like Jesus. Some things are worth living for. Some things are worth dying for. Jesus is the ultimate soldier. He became a necessary evil. He became sin (2 Cor 5:21). Donating Himself as a ritual sin-offering in order to purify all human life through and through, He transformed Himself into a dumpster for the

---

24. Incidentally, royalties of this book are directed to the *Wounded Warriors Canada* organization in support of soldiers and veterans who continue to bear the consequences of sacrifices made overseas.

refuse of earthly iniquity and spiritual brokenness; a viperous devil on a cruciform pole sucking away the poison of human tragedy, drinking the death of the world's carcass; an imploding mine with infinitely more annihilating capabilities than the most destructive atomic bomb. Yet though He had no sin, and was not responsible for any of the evils of the world, He willingly suffered the consequences of our human crimes, selfishness, fear and lack of repentance, by the roasting of His flesh on the altar of the cross. The divine incarnational experience is without comparison. Do *I* really have the audacity to compare myself with *Him*? I am not *that* arrogant, I hope. And this God continued to forgive Debby her trespasses in the same way as He continues to forgive each one of us too. I was persuaded to do the same.

Debby taught me a lot about the feebleness of my faith as a pastor; how I required little help from the devil in despising my divine call. None of us are immune to envy. All of us are susceptible to jealousy. In my case, my skillful way of construing facts in justification of self-preservation and driven by self-love had convinced me that a blessed God-given vocation to rescue this lost lamb was somehow beneath my self-worth. Even though I knew that a pastor's scepter was a towel,[25] my heart insisted that I deserved better than this. No one is ever content in the outpost; each one craves the center stage.[26] But there is only room for one. And yet He disappears into the crevices aspiring to serve those with whom they are infested—namely each one of us. Jesus does not share our lascivious career objectives for promotion to the next level of incompetency.[27] Our Lord stayed where He was, and did what He was commissioned to do with unhindered dedication to one singular self-sacrificial mission. Society resides in the illusion that it inhabits higher places. Personifying spiritual antipathy, I, for one, still depravedly believe that I am entitled to more. It's a confession, not an excuse. In the West we consume. Often our "innocent" consumption occurs at the

---

25. LSB 857.

26. Incidentally, in organizations like the military sometimes those who require the most surveillance and management find themselves in headquarters, whereas the most trustworthy soldiers remain in isolated postings. The popular and famous evangelists in the eyes of Christians are not necessarily the greatest in the Kingdom of God (Matt 18:1–5).

27. In management theory, the *Peter's Principle* states that the selection of candidates for promotion is based on their performance in their current roles, rather than on abilities relevant to the intended roles. Thus, managers rise to the level of their incompetence, making them not more efficient in their work, but less (at least in the short run). In short, we are most effective at what we have already learned to do.

Who's Afraid of the Steppenwolf?

expense of crippled ethnic children in sweat shops that parallel the hostile conditions captured in a Charles Dickens' novel. Oh well: out of sight; out of mind.

But physical possessions are not our only obsession. Accumulating *experiences* is a major contributor to the lengthening bucket lists in our hoarding society that has everything it needs, bursting the top off Maslow's hierarchy of needs. Yet, discontented, we still want more. The devil may tempt us with evil but he also influences us with things good and innocent. For me as a young man, a love of the diversity of God's marvelous creation, and an insatiable desire for discovery through travel, became that without which I could not live, characterizing my identity at the expense of the definition and vocabulary established by God's Word. Circumscribing oneself in terms other than the Word of God is nothing less than idolatry. Abandoning one's station in life amounts to running away from God, replicating the hankerings of unsatisfied demons fleeing from their God-given callings. Roman sentries who abandoned their post were executed as deserters. Even well-meaning soldiers engaging in a preemptive strike were considered traitors in their clumsy exposure of the defensive system to enemy attack. Most of their armour was defensive, with the sole exception of their double-edged sword. Our only weapon is the sword of the Word grasped with hands of prayer as we guard holy ground.[28] The territory that we have been called to cover may, for one, be framed by the boring walls of an office cubicle or, for another, be delineated by the plain bleached sheets of a hospital bed. Yet in each particular posting, the Holy Spirit engages in spiritual war through Christian sentries who pray, speak and love. Accordingly, the devil assiduously impels us to detest these posts, whatever our stations in life may happen to be.

The prophet Jonah holds no patent on vocational desertion. In my younger years I viewed God's beautiful world as a fascinating playground awaiting exploration. Stated more crudely, I saw it as a smorgasbord of endless possible experiences enticing me to eat to my gluttonous fill. But instead of being contented with sampling the generous portions already offered to me, I wanted to pig-out on everything, even eyeing the leftovers on other people's plates. As I age and mature ever so slowly in my faith, I concede this covetous ambition as the worship of creation and of self. We want what isn't ours. We always want more. While most people try to survive on a dollar a day, the demented and luxurious belief that I was missing out in

---

28. See Kleinig, *Grace upon Grace: Spirituality for Today*, 256–260.

a self-engineered race to see it all, dictated the trajectory of my life's goals. The Christian aphorism that we have been placed in this world not to serve self but others had become extraneous to my spirituality. Indeed, God has a plan for each of us, but His call that we pick up our cross and follow Jesus usually has little to do with satisfying feelings of self-fulfillment, making our dreams come true, marrying the most attractive partner, and changing the world by making a name for ourselves. Serving Debby was my calling at that particular moment. It was not just something to be tolerated. It was an occasion to rejoice. I was, after all, *exactly where God wanted me to be.* That promise ought to have sufficed. Since then, I have developed a hunch that on the other side we will discover that what we thought was of greatest of import counted for very little, and that what we despised as trivial will be reckoned to be of utmost significance. Debby offered me an opportunity to gaze into the stunning face of grace; an occasion to multiply the bread of forgiveness. For what more could a pastor wish?

The magnitude of the rhetorical question, "If God kept a record of sins, who could stand?" (Ps 130:3) struck home after the suicide of a friend of mine as a young adult. A committed Christian, but mentally unstable, he was derogatorily classified as a "suicide waiting to happen." I was the last one he saw before he took his life. I told him that I would pray for him—so much for personal victories—for both of us. I was tormented by doubts. Had he stumbled into hell because he failed to repent of his sins before he drew his last breath? Does one's eternal destiny hang upon the timeliness of one's final confession? What happens when a substantial degree of attrition is prominent? Does the lack of pure unadulterated contrition on a Christian's deathbed cripple the promises of God sealed at Holy Baptism? I suppose purgatory poses a convenient solution: an opportunity to address those forgotten sins and neglected confessions. But it seems out of character with a God who says that He freely acquits not only our cups of sin confessed, but also the ocean of those of which we are unaware. I may be wrong. Nonetheless, the cousins of disappointment and suffering parade alongside the Christian march. But to think too much of one's own spiritual excursion is to lose sight of the leader of the expedition, with His cross as a pole and the Book of Life as a flag, since "All personal triumph or success, despair or failure becomes irrelevant if we suffer God's own suffering."[29] Instead, as Lutheran pastor and devotional writer Dietrich Bonhoeffer continues, one strives to have "one's thoughts swept far beyond one's own per-

---

29. Bonhoeffer, *Meditations on the Cross*, 38.

sonal fate to the ultimate meaning of all life and suffering, and of whatever occurs, such that one is seized by a great hope."[30]

In spite of all efforts to hide her, the Blessed Virgin Mary remains a picture of the body of Christ. If we have difficulty imagining the hardships of Christ because He was perfect, then imagine those of Mary, the icon of the Church. She is not co-mediatrix in salvation, but she does assist us in our spiritual journey as she personifies the tragic drawbacks of following Jesus: personal disappointment. Flesh of her flesh, butchered and nailed like a piece of meat to a pole. Except when lack of maternal instinct or irate selfishness results in the willful termination of pregnancy, every mother would gladly take the place of her suffering child. None wish to outlive their babies. We are given no choices in matters of suffering. We are only asked to accept, or better yet, embrace them. Certainly, suffering evil does not make one more holy—otherwise the devil, the prince of hell, would be the godliest among us—but it is a divine tool. After all, "the safest road to hell is the gradual one—the gentle slope, soft underfoot, without sudden turnings, without milestones, without signposts."[31] Moreover, God doesn't only work through suffering *sometimes*. He does so *always*. Michelangelo's *The Pieta* is not intended to inspire, but to remind. We will be disappointed: our expectations, too demanding; our dreams, too costly. We are wise to never forget that when we feel ourselves to be out of place and unhappy in life, it is no accident that we are where we are. The world is a sinful mess. What is remarkable is that God chooses to use us to help clean it up.

+ + +

The Bible reminds us that not all suffering is on account of our faith, though God will use it all for our benefit. Later I discovered that some of Debby's suffering was self-inflicted. God is very generous. One curiosity about Debby's continued backsliding into the occult was the role played by sex. In my limited experience with the satanic arts, I have observed how abuses of sex, drugs, and the occult are associated. God seems to concur. *The Epistle to the Galatians* expels a list of "sins of the flesh" (Gal 5:20). One of them, *pharmakia* (from which we receive "pharmacy"), is translated as "sorcery of magic" in some English versions, but also as "drugs and incantations" elsewhere. *The Revelation of St. John* denounces the same practices

30. Ibid.
31. Lewis, *The Screwtape Letters*, 39.

(Rev 9:21, 21:8 and 22:15). The concept of "root poisons" that were used to cause abortions is found in various Hebrew literature and echoes the New Testament word. Other Christian literature uses the identical word in reference not only to the wilful termination of pregnancies, but also to contraception; two notions closely interwoven with black and white magic because of the methods by which they were employed: normally administered along with pagan blessings.[32] These sins are often clustered together indicating their intricate relationship. The grouping is not random. This should come of no surprise to us. Sex is intended, primarily, for reproduction and always within the institution of a marriage. Some Jews, many Christians, and most Muslims understand that contraception amounts to redefining the terms of sex from those of reproduction to those of pleasure.

Today, sexual organs are often tragically regarded as accidents of the human body and no longer essential to our being. Neither are they esteemed as an intimate extension of individual creative energies and an instrument of loving service in their reproduction of life. Monogamous marriage and procreation of children are nothing less than a participation in the excitement and joy of creation experienced by the community of the Holy Trinity. No wonder the devil detests it so. It ought to come as no shock then that the millennial generation has reached unprecedented heights in the categories of sexual confusion and crisis of identity. Human beings long for joy, strive for happiness, and settle for pleasure. If sin can be defined as the incorrigible human desire and capacity to turn inwards upon oneself (e.g. by serving oneself as opposed to others), then the popular disdain of God's first commandment and promise given to His first human creatures before their plummet into sin, which is to replenish the earth within the parameters of heterosexual marriage, represents an idolatry of pleasure. It also represents a demonic twisting of sexuality as self-fulfilling. Reproduction is obviously essential to the survival of the human race. But Christian babies populate heaven. The delightfully intimate gift of sexual pleasure, which is an unnecessary but welcome side-effect indeed, does not preclude its instrumentality. In other words, it is a means, not an end. In Augustinian language, if God is the only true "end" to be enjoyed, then all things for "use" when treated as "ends" are, by definition, demonic idolatrous imitations of Him. When sex itself is treated as the goal it becomes a false God, to whom many in contemporary culture pretentiously pay great homage and worship. Even Babylonian temple prostitution went part and parcel

---

32. Riddle, *Eve's Herbs: A History of Contraception and Abortion in the West*, 65.

with fertility rites. But today, the devil has convinced us that fertility is not a blessed condition, but rather a cursed one. Large families are viewed as odd, even disdained. What sort of diabolical masochistic spirit spurns the gifts of God and banishes children as disruptive to a happy life? Babies are a gift from God, "the fruit of the womb a reward" (Ps 127:3b). We choose contraception. Sometimes we murder them, or, as Christians we attempt with Pilate to wash our hands of the guilt. Every birth in fact is typological of the Christ child, who proves to be our greatest inconvenience. We murdered Him too. And yet the Holy Spirit draws some back. The Father waits with open arms, along with all the slaughtered holy innocents of His coming kingdom. In the meantime the goddesses of contraception and abortion offer "salvation" not only from parental and societal responsibility, but also from being fully human; euphonically in tune with the demonic frequency of loathing our "creatureliness." If this reasoning is correct, then fornication and pornography, for instance, are not only sinful, but portals for demons. Debby is a compelling example.

Without suggesting a hierarchy of sins in terms of their eternal consequences, a distinction endures between participating willingly or unwillingly in any given sin. The Roman categorization of venial and mortal sins attempts to sharpen the distinction, but can easily lead to a downplaying of the gravity of *all* sin as well as belittling the depravity of the sinful condition entirely. Sins are equally unholy, but the consequences are different when, say, we act on our sinful thoughts. Believing that the magnitude of committing any particular "venial" sin is slight changes nothing. When people defend their pet sins as harmless by arguing that they are not hurting anybody else, they neglect to appreciate the profound importance of their instrumentality to God in shaping and changing our world. In other words, all sins are not only self-destructive but make us less useful in serving others. Yes, reading a dirty magazine hurts one's neighbours.

It is startling how much internet time is devoted to browsing pornographic material.[33] Pornography changes the way that one views not only the opposite sex, but oneself in specific and God's creation in general. It is adultery and fornication of a kind, for, oddly enough, the image becomes the sexual companion. Marriages are shattered due to the lie that interacting with these unseemly pictures is harmless. Even if the encounter is limited to the eyes, the relationship can be compared to a love affair. Though

---

33. Exactly how much internet time is devoted to porn is difficult to substantiate. Statistics of porn-related web searches range from fifteen to thirty-five percent.

so obviously artificial, the devil persists in his skilled impersonations. Otherwise anorexia would not have such a powerful hold on masses of women struggling with issues of self-image. Breasts are intended to produce breast milk; their size makes no difference. Today's standards for beauty are sheer fantasy, and yet we have convinced ourselves that, with plastic surgeries, trendy fashion and grotesque eating habits, they are somewhat achievable. The novels of Gustave Flaubert persuasively exhibit the extent to which masculine passion obsesses in striving for an unattainable and imaginary love.

In the sadistic adult playground of Debby's world, "love-making" happened in an artificial environment while under the influence of illegal drugs where even the shadows of true love are subjugated to the dark desires of blighted and inured hearts. She was often appallingly unconscious and unfamiliar with the identity of her partners the morning after. For addicts and the curious alike, the faces on the internet are only strangers, and easily forgotten, but the demonic damage is done. Memories remain. The digital images linger, engraved, provoking a plethora of unreal subconscious utopian expectations and distorted imaginations regarding possibilities in the relationships between normal human couples. There may be no risk of pregnancy, disease or the shame of being exposed, but the idols stay hidden in the most resigned closets of hearts. They make their appearances at untimely moments, sometimes invited by their owners. Accordingly, we do not require the devil to tempt us; we have mastered the art ourselves. We treasure our idols. There is no end to their magnanimity, until they are smashed by the hammer of the cross through the incontrovertible words of confession and the holy absolution. Yet even then, there are marks that ache, wounds that itch. Thankfully not all scars are humiliating and painful reminders. Cain receives a mark to buffer him from danger, although no promise of his safety is guaranteed (Gen 4:15). Yet Jacob, after wrestling with the God-man figure in the desert, and refusing to let go of this friend (despite direful appearances to the contrary) departs with a permanent limp; a humble reminder to this patriarch that God is in charge (Gen 32:31). After all, "we know that for those who love God all things work together for good" (Rom 8:28). Even Jesus has scars, as our *eternal* reminder of His love for His Father, and the extremes that He underwent to have us with Him, at His side, in His Kingdom.

Who's Afraid of the Steppenwolf?

+ + +

The first exorcism of Debby's demon was definitely the worst of all. After that, the sessions were longer and emotionally draining, but I increasingly felt more confident. I knew what to expect. God had proven Himself once, and He would do it again. I was His child after all. And after baptizing Debby, more "tools" were available to me. For those disturbed, frightened or damaged by the horrors of past events, the laying on of hands and anointing with oil helps. Debby was no exception. Sometimes the demon required some prying, reluctant to unmask itself. I found it rather strange, *invoking,* or even *awakening,* the menacing demon in this possessed child of God. Some formulas for exorcism command the evil minions to tell by some sign their names, ordering them to obey the exorcist's words to the letter. In my case it did not take much persuasion. I didn't even need a name; "unclean spirit" worked fine. The Good News was that Debby now belonged to Jesus. She had been taken just as she was "without one plea,"[34] all her unattractive faults included. And no matter how hard he tried, the devil could not have her back. She was eventually instructed for the Sacrament of the Altar. I still picture her on the day of her first communion, wobbling up the church steps with our elderly elders propping her up on both sides; a cruciform trinity of brokenness buttressed by old age, but all of them eager to partake in a feast fit for kings. All personal distinctions dissolved in this most intimate fellowship between God and His Church, bearing the weight of the body together. We are all identical, in that we each eat the same heavenly bread and drink the same heavenly drink. Each of us lives between the font and the cup. Old and young, rich and poor, mentally stable and unstable, emotional wrecks and those who cope fine, all stand together as beggars; equally hungering for righteousness and thirsting for grace, united in a shared longing for healing and hope.[35] Although repeated daily and weekly, Holy Communion occurs only once, a timeless liturgy sung in unison at the footsteps of the gateway to paradise, transcending all times and all places with a beauty and glory that surpasses all superficial distinctions. As many grains become one loaf, we, who are many, become one single body—His holy body. Although we see through a mirror dimly, "You are what you eat."

---

34. LSB 570.
35. Walther, *God Grant It,* 337.

My First Exorcism

+ + +

Many years have passed since I shepherded that flock in that broken yet blessed parish. I have recently researched Debby's status, and it turns out that she died of a mortal stroke. Over time, and after witnessing countless tragedies and episodes of grief in the life of his sheep, a pastor is sure to develop the impression that God is more interested in our company in heaven than we are which is likely why He has made salvation so easy and completed all the necessary work Himself. Counterproductively, like a drowning swimmer slapping away the salutary hand of the lifeguard, we continually find toilsome ways to complicate our rescue, with some help from the evil foe no doubt. God's grace, then, must be "sufficient" (2 Cor 12:9) otherwise we would be entirely without hope. Debby's shortened lifespan was a gift from above, as God benevolently captured her, not only from her grotesque temptations and tragic calamities of life, but also from the asylum of herself. Happily now she sleeps in Jesus. Having no family, the congregation became her closest relations during her last years on earth. The pastor was her father; fellow believers, her brothers and sisters; the Church, her mother. Christ's blood is thicker and richer than all genetic blood ties. She has joined her true siblings with our heavenly Father in glory, a saint among the angels, and archangels and all the company of heaven.

It will be overwhelmingly rewarding for the Lord's ministers when we ourselves are carried to our heavenly home, to bear witness to the stunning masses of lives that we were instrumental in touching and saving—lots of surprises I suspect. On earth, we often miss the delightful opportunity to observe seeds planted by the Lord's holy ministry grow and multiply; especially pastors who do not remain many years in the same parish. But in the kingdom of glory the harvest will have been completed. For we stewards of the mysteries, when we arrive into paradise, will not await a beach full of virgins attending to all of our short-lived sensual and selfish pleasures.[36] Eternal life will be immeasurably better. Instead, we will worship the Lamb on His throne forever! Unbelievers would be disappointed with such a heaven, one that is not designed to satisfy their earthly cravings paralleling treasures stored on earth (Matt 6:19–21). Thus, those in hell are precisely where they belong. Theoretically they would be uncomfortable in heaven, spending eternity with the God that they found unpalatable before death.

---

36. Many Muslims understand heaven in terms of the fulfilment of sensual pleasure such as the reward of seventy-two virgins per male inhabitant.

Forcing them into a bond of wedlock with a body that they abhor is nothing other than rape.[37] Having tasted the divine love on earth and rejected it, heaven would become their hell—just ask the demons. They willingly left God's presence because they no longer belonged. "As you live, so you die."

Incidentally, Debby's pastor confided to me that even up to his last visit with her, she struggled with demonic bondage. He recounted how, as he had read her Holy Scripture, she began to shuffle nervously, awkwardly lowering her head until she irrepressibly shouted, "Shut up!" A short instant later, the evil receded as she reestablished her composure. With a delicate and gratified child-like smile spread across her sickly pale yet blissful face, she delightfully stated, "It's gone. I feel peace," while asking her pastor to continue with his prayers. Debby's stubborn impudence was her most admirable quality. An already dried-out heart is not easily broken, and Debby was spiritually tough. Some Christians believe that the Christian walk is either "all" or "nothing." One is either "hot" or "cold." For them it is inconceivable how one could reside as both a sinner and saint, simultaneously. Moreover, it is easy to judge those who continue to struggle with a particular temptation that we scrutinize as unfamiliar to our personal experience, such as a substance abuse and addiction. However, each person wrestles with his or her own secret struggles, burdens that often last a lifetime. Spiritual mediocrity taints the prayers of *all* the faithful. The legacy of Adam destines each of us as forlorn:

> For I know that nothing good dwells in me, that is, in my flesh. For I have the desire to do what is right, but not the ability to carry it out. For I do not do the good I want, but the evil I do not want is what I keep on doing (Rom 7:18–19).

Yet it is not the most wretched thing in the world to battle with the same infernal vice throughout one's life. At the very least, it keeps one humble. Do not misunderstand me. Every Christian desires to subdue sins. But to believe that we *have* overcome one, and that we can now wash our hands of it while we stroke it off the bucket list entitled "Temptations to Beat Before Expiration" while we move on to the next item in the inventory, does not resonate well with honest human experience. There are, after all, only ten Commandments: a short, yet conclusive list. Worse than struggling with

---

37. Some Christians who question the existence of hell as a place argue that hell is paradise experienced by a condemned soul. While offering an attractive alternative to the "fire and brimstone" it seems out of character with the mercy of God who forces no one to remain in His kingdom.

the same sin is the belief that you have already conquered it—and all others like it. A sincere acknowledgement of our inauspicious weakness, an acceptance of a lifelong handicap, drives us to an alertness which protects us from the clever strategies of the devil. A soldier maximizes his effectiveness in battle when actively conscientious of his own weakness. The belief that we progress in our spiritual journey, improving our ascent up the rungs of the ladder of holiness, is shattered by an honest account of the state of our soul. Truly we remain completely sinners, aliens to righteousness.

On the bright side, we are also saints. We have been made God's children, covered by the robe of righteousness of the only holy and perfect One, Jesus: our Jacob's ladder (John 1:51). As a result, we convicted criminals have been declared "not guilty." We have been sealed with the signet ring of His Spirit (Rev 9:4). We belong to Christ, protected from the tampering of the devil, hidden in the shadow of our charitable and merciful Lord's wings (Ps 17:8b). The vilest sinner wins the reward of the holiest saint as all trifling scales of moralistic perfection are levelled under those earth-shattering words, "It is finished." Consequentially, the repugnant odour of the filthy rags of all of our good deeds has become a fragrant perfume (Eph 5:2) in the presence of God, drenched with the blood of our Lord and Saviour. Just as fresh clean clothes on a newly bathed infant makes the child smell better, so too, the robe of Christ's righteousness after our baptismal bath endows us with a new scent and changes our lives.

At the end of John Bunyan's *Pilgrim's Progress*, the battered and worn-out Christian is amazed to find out that *God* had been carrying him past all of his pitfalls. It was actually Christ's journey, not his. So too, *we* get carried along a journey that is less about us than we may like to think. It is, however, an exhausting vertical climb up the steep cliff of the Law when we insist on tackling it alone. Our common experience in life resembles that of Hermann Hesse's *Steppenwolf*. We perceive ourselves as good, and yet there is an undeniable wicked wolf residing inside each one of us. Even pious Christians should not become overly shocked by the dark wickedness that hides within them. The self consists of two natures—sinner and saint—simultaneously present; the two intricately intermingled like a treacherous climbing vine wrapped tightly around an otherwise healthy plant. The Old Adam must, therefore, by "daily contrition and repentance be drowned and die with all sins and evil desires."[38] He is to be subdued at each moment throughout the day. True Christianity then is teaching people not how to

---

38. LSB 325.

live, but how to die. An evening prayer, recorded by eighteenth-century theologian and Pastor, Johann Konrad Wilhelm Löhe, underscores the provocative and unsettling response to this destiny:

> Lord Jesus Christ, Prince of Life, humbly do I beseech Thee to grant me the grace of Thy Holy Spirit, that I may live this life not unto self, but alone unto Thy glory; that I may consider every moment, what it is to die, and what comes afterward for both the wicked and the good; that ere mine hour cometh I may have learned how to die, and always practice what I have so learned; that I may finally depart from this world's pilgrimage unto the fatherland in heaven. Amen.[39]

The victorious life that many Christians believe can be realized on earth and in time, is a demonic lie. We are all far less holy than we think. The walk of faith ought to be characterized, not as a vivacious muscular soldier persevering through boot camp, but as a frail ill patient undergoing palliative care. Christianity is not a religious oasis but a spiritual battlefield. One of the founding fathers of American Lutheranism, C.F.W. Walther, writes,

> Those who confess that they are almost never entirely free from the trial, care, and sorrow of the heart are in a happy condition. . . . Without misery about sin and sorrow of their heart, they would never remain in Christ. Instead they would soon become secure, proud and self-righteous. The sorrow with which they are continually visited is the means God employs to keep them with Christ.[40]

+ + +

One catechumen of mine, who was struggling with demonic subjection, rejected the sacrament of Holy Baptism after hearing that he would inevitably continue to sin thereafter. We remain sinners. Therefore we sin. "What then was the use of baptism?" he reasoned. "Isn't Christianity about my internal transformation?" This new convert was hampered from celebrating the tremendously freeing corollaries of the gleeful doctrine of justification: that one's status is changed before God through a forensic declaration announced and offered at Holy Baptism. Despite appearances,

---

39. Löhe, *Seed Grains of Prayer: a Manual for evangelical Christians*, 52–53.
40. Walther, *God Grant It*, 391.

we *are* holy. We *are* loved. There is nothing more that we can add, do or contribute to that glorious pronouncement. Instead, this troubled soul saw faith and love as substances infused into the heart through the Sacrament which, over a lifetime, grow in accordance with an arbitrary and subjective scale of measurement. "If you do your very best, almighty God will do the rest," jingles the medieval Roman rhyme. But what happens when the accumulation of one's good works is below average? Modest-minded Christians can never be certain whether or not they are truly saved. Does pure philanthropy, with no ulterior motives, actually exist?

On another occasion, a new Asian immigrant to Canada refused Holy Baptism after I explained that, despite a new peace, hope and salvation, his life on earth would only become more taxing as a Christian. After all, the devil wages war upon his enemies, not his friends. We inherit a cross. How many Christians foster false expectations in believing that their lives will simply improve after conversion? How many missionaries win souls for Christ with the sales pitch that God will fix all of their problems, appeasing crowds with an "opium of the people" as Karl Marx observed? A victorious life on earth characterized by an enormous pile of personal moral successes denies the consequences of the sin adjacent to our every thought, word and deed. Instead, victory is a hope to be realized in eternity. As the parable of the weeds among the wheat suggests, a premature harvest of the weeds from the wheat is not only unkind to potential converts who are deprived of an opportunity to repent before Armageddon, it is also dangerous to Christians who need not look far in observing the suffocating grip of ungodly weeds intermingled throughout the fabric of their spirits. An immediate pruning may be to our detriment. The forgiveness of sins is always the safer bet.

The most decisive theological and philosophical error of our time is the belief that we deserve more from life. Why is it that Christians expect that all will go well when it is *the cross* that molds the motif for our metaphysics? Satan tempted Jesus with the riches, glory and lust of this world. If He undergoes such trials immediately after His baptism, what evil proclivity compels us sinful malefactors to think that we would escape them after our own? Jesus is the only one deserving of anything good, and yet forgoes it all. Justice is not grace. People who are hired last get paid the same.[41] God is generous. We are jealous. The unfairness of God reflects that He loves us enough to be unfair, otherwise Jesus would never have agreed to come from

---

41. Petersen, *Thy Kingdom Come*, 4.

heaven to earth. Divine fairness is not in our vested interests. The number of bad things that occur in a day should come of no surprise to us—but the good things should. This is a miracle. This is grace. God is so eager to answer our prayers that He even answers an indefinite multitude of them before we have the chance to pray. Amiably secluded from inauspicious potentialities through petitions from our omnipotent intercessor who prevents them from ever occurring, we remain oblivious to Jesus' unceasing supplications. He neither slumbers nor sleeps (Ps 121:4) living to make intercession for us (Heb 7:25). This too is a miracle. This too is grace.

Many Protestants and Romanists severely criticize Luther's axiomatic anthropological principle of *simul iustus et peccator* due to their own nuances on sanctification, even to the point of accusing Lutherans of antinomianism. It seems rather extreme and exaggerated. However, theological accents can easily develop into ideologies. The Lutheran Church does not deny regeneration and the radical impact that the Holy Spirit has in changing our lives displayed through acts of piety and good works. But it can become a very perilous trend to focus on one's own spiritual progression at the expense of a faltering perception of oneself as the greatest of spiritual beggars. Sinister seeds of self-security sprout into trees of self-righteousness.

According to the aforesaid paradigm, Christ simply becomes useful to self-development while issues of salvation are shelved away. False religion believes that the evils of the world are found outside of oneself, and not inside. True religion blames the self. And if humility provides the shape for our journey, then the point of celebrating one's own achievements is a moot one. Boasting is usually counterproductive. The branches of a healthy tree bloom into delicious fruit *for others* to eat. Such fruit lasts forever, a beautifying harvest following it into paradise (Rev 14:13). God is well-pleased with the freshness of fruits from His vineyard that breathes forth heavenly fragrances (Gen 27:27). True good works are God's. Thus they are eternal. However, the moment a tree begins to bend its branch towards itself for nourishment, narcissistically chewing upon its own fruit through, say, self-admiration, self-love, and even introspective humility, that tree annuls its divinely ordained purpose: to serve its neighbour.[42] Instead something demonic and demented takes place.

---

42. As the parable of the talents warn, those who hoard their faith away for selfish purposes, crippling its intended use, which is to increase and bear fruit, are "worthless" and fit only for "outer darkness" where "there will be weeping and gnashing of teeth" (Matt 25:14–30).

My First Exorcism

To help us lose ourselves in the enveloping righteousness of Christ and Him crucified, most of our good works remain shrouded in darkness until they are unveiled in all their splendour and glory on Judgment Day (1 Cor 4:1–5). The Bible is God's story, not ours; an epic account of His self-denial, not our own. Bonhoeffer articulates it in the following way:

> When we have completely renounced trying to make something of ourselves, then we completely throw ourselves in God's arms, take God's own suffering in the world seriously rather than our own, and keep watch with Christ in Gethsemane. That, I think, is faith. That is conversion, and it is in this way that one becomes a human being, a Christian.[43]

Bonhoeffer wrote these words from the Tegel prison in 1944 after his involvement in the unsuccessful plot to assassinate Adolf Hitler, for which he was later executed. He knew that he was about to die (which is what I suspect he meant by his reference to Gethsemane) and that he deserved nothing better as he strove to recognize himself as inferior to others. All this is antithetical to self-conceit, or what is more popularly called "self-esteem." He masterfully echoes the attitude of St. Paul who states that he is the worst of all sinners (1 Tim 1:15–16) which, by the way, was written *after* his conversion and not before. St. Paul carried that "negating" self-assessment with himself all the way to the grave, despite the liberal judgments of other fellow believers who likely hailed, "Oh brother Paul, you are exaggerating. You are too modest. You are such a morally outstandingly good man"...etc. Bonhoeffer professes his nothingness elsewhere:

> If my sinfulness appears to me to be in any way smaller or less detestable in comparison with the sin of others, I am still not recognizing my sinfulness at all. My sin is of necessity the worst, the most grievous, the most reprehensible. Brotherly love will find any number of extenuations for the sins of others; only for my sin is there no apology whatsoever. Therefore my sin is the worst. He who would serve his brother in the fellowship must sink all the way down to these depths of humility. How can I possibly serve another person in unfeigned humility if I seriously regard his sinfulness as worse than my own?[44]

Victorian novelist, Anne Brontë's *The Tenant of Wildfell Hall* describes the unsettling changes that occur within the matrimonial union of two

---

43. Bonhoeffer, *Meditations on the Cross*, 38.
44. Bonhoeffer, *Life Together*, 97.

morally unequal lovers; one a pure-hearted and prayerful romantic, and the other a hedonistic belligerent alcoholic. The protagonist is stunned and horrified by how what she once found to be repulsive behaviour had become rather normal to her moral palette. Reminiscing over her innocent years, she wonders whether she was too severe in her judgments regarding good and bad. It is her way of coping with her new self—the fact that this beastly man has become one with her—and having now to share his degradations, failings and trespasses. Though she herself is without blame, she now blushes at all his ignominy and cannot help but defend and make excuses for them, and for him. In becoming one flesh their identities and sins become entangled and interlinked.

Similarly, as a sinner, we have consummated our marriage with the evil one in our conception. Whether or not we had any choice in the union is irrelevant. We have inherited all kinds of indignation. We are contaminated. What we find appalling in others often represents the traits that we hate most about ourselves. Any aberration that we identify outside, in the world, can also be found invading the frames of our own hearts. Personal shame is, perhaps, the explanation for why opposites attract. Yet we have been remarried anew by a Lord who is well acquainted with of all of our faults. He gains little in the spiritual matrimonial relationship created through the rite of Holy Baptism and consummated through His Holy Supper, yet only fully solidified in the wedding festivities reserved for heaven. For now, we continue to live pursued by an abusive and violating ex-spouse who requires constant reminders of the conditions of his restraining order. This is what the battle with the old Adam, the devil, flesh and sinful nature entails. As neo-Marxist philosopher Hannah Arendt has pointed out, although the human condition may change, our human nature does not. We all share an identical spiritual predicament. We come in packages of all sorts of sizes, shapes and colours but the wiring within is essentially the same.

The forgiveness of sins is a forgiveness of guilt. Our pregnancy with original sin affects every one of our moods and behaviours. The effects of sin linger on, and strictly speaking, the sin stays as well. Justification by grace means that God *considers us righteous* because He has removed the imputation of our sin, even though the substance of original sin still remains. Perhaps an illustration can clarify the point. If a clumsy child breaks an expensive ceramic vase, his parent pays for the damage. His mom and dad relieve him of his guilt, atoning for his sin, in a sense. But the mess of shattered glass does not magically disappear. Although we are forgiven, we remain sinners who dwell alongside the consequences of our sins. We sin because we are sinners. We are not sinners because we sin. If we were not chronic sinners, we would not die, since the wages of sin is death (Rom 6:23). Yet we all *do* die and we are all dying. We ought not to be surprised then that the demons continue their vicious onslaughts against ex-occultists who have since been adopted into the kingdom of light. At times, as was the case with Debby, they may even repossess them. "The spirit is indeed willing, but the flesh is weak" (Matt 26:41b).

If God's grace is insufficient for salvation, we are all without hope. Besides, forms of martyrdom and the cross are promised to all of His children, especially in the latter days. A theology of glory that boasts the Christian as a spiritual hero—healthy, wealthy and happy—either promotes self-righteousness or, conversely, leads honest souls into despair. Plagued by temptation, seventeenth-century Lutheran pastor Johann Gerhard confesses that before the devil

> casts me headlong into sin, he persuades me that sin is lighter than a feather, lighter than a leaf on the air. As soon as he casts me headlong into sin, he repeatedly asserts that sin is greater than heaven and earth and heavier than the balance of divine mercy.[45]

Efforts to obey the divine Law never deliver the promised goods. Perpetuating a faith in false hopes and dreams insinuates that God has not kept His covenant. Faith loses its foundation and becomes, instead, a Kierkegaardian leap of wishful hope into the unknown, with fingers crossed behind the back. The value of faith is pegged in the process of believing. Faith turns inward upon itself—faith becomes the object of faith! Such faith amounts to a fatal fall into a dark abyss of a religion of man's own creation. One is tossed into a confession of a God who shows favouritism. At best, the Christian's refuge becomes an appeal to divine sovereignty or God's hidden will. At worst, God is viewed as toying with us.

C.F.W. Walther observed that when the ground of our faith rests upon our own goodness, happy experiences, temporal blessings, other people's opinions of us, or vacillating personal feelings, this sandy foundation crumbles away when the waves of tribulation strike or the dark winters of doubt arrive.[46] Our positive feelings are exposed as a delusion; our geniality revealed to be lacking; our happy experiences replaced with tragedy.

---

45. Gerhard, *Meditations on Divine Mercy*, 124.
46. Walther, *God Grant It*, 147.

Who's Afraid of the Steppenwolf?

Faith must be founded on the correct cornerstone. When I was a kid, I heard about a deluded boy who jumped off the roof of his house because he believed that he was superman. He had a lot of faith—in the wrong thing. Power and authority are not identical. I would rather lack power and even faith, and still own authority over the kingdom of darkness, than have no authority, but boast a powerful faith. For instance, when preaching sermons, pastors are wise to sparsely use the word "faith." Talking about faith never creates faith. But talking about Jesus does. Likewise, sermons on the Holy Spirit tend to juxtapose Him from the work of Christ. Instead, the Holy Spirit desires to remain the silent person of the Holy Trinity, whose role it is to create faith in Jesus Christ, the Way to the heavenly Father. Faith does not create faith. But God's Word does.

Neither do miracles, in and of themselves, create faith. We inadvertently commiserate with the singer's demand in the rock opera, *Jesus Christ Superstar*, "Jesus Christ, if you're divine, turn my water into wine. Prove to me that you're no fool, walk across my swimming pool." Yet curiously, after Jesus exorcizes the demons in Luke chapter eight, the people ask Him to leave them alone. When Jesus finishes feeding thousands, most of His disciples abandon Him (John 6:66). Even after His resurrection, some of them still have doubts. Miracles are acts of victory over the forces of nature that oppose us, but they do not in themselves create faith in the Son of God. Similarly, personal victories do not create faith. To my surprise, the lack of overarching temporal victory in the case of Debby had been a hidden blessing in my pastoral ministry. As is the case concerning all the afflictions of a shepherd's sheep, they afford the pastor endless occasions for prayer to a heavenly Father who is more ready to give than we are to ask.

Likewise, the injustices that we experience provide priceless opportunities to forgive. In the act of forgiveness we learn more about ourselves and God, than we do about those who offend us. Christ's *kenosis* or "emptying of Himself" is reciprocated in our own. True unconditional forgiveness is a self-emptying that challenges us to hurdle over the argument that it is unwise, deriding childish requirements of visible displays of gratitude, repentance or contrition. "For with the judgment you pronounce you will be judged, and with the measure you use it will be measured to you" (Matt 7:2).

Forgiveness is the only way to step over these bleak walls of conditions and suspicions that we have guardedly—and even unknowingly—established. In the place of resentment and revenge we welcome others into our lives without expecting anything in return. The compassionate Father has daringly and impetuously welcomed us into His benevolent heart in spite of a conclusive and thorough knowledge of every evil inclination and antipathy of our own. He even calls us enemies His friends. Even better, He makes us beloved children. The unattainability of a perfect imitation of this kind of love cannot be an excuse for only begrudgingly exonerating the faults of the other.

Debby was certainly sorry for all the abuse to which she exposed her pastor, even though she was reluctant to state the obvious. Whether overtaken by the intensity of guilt or the impertinence of pride, most people rarely say that they are sorry. No one does it all the time. It is easy to highlight the neglect of others whom we are not enthusiastic to forgive anyways, and tightly tie our forgiveness to their utterance of the words, "I am sorry. . .please forgive me." In reflecting upon the famous Rembrandt painting, *Return of the Prodigal Son*, the Canadian devotional writer, Henri Nouwen, who devoted his life to working with the mentally-challenged, writes:

> I have often said, "I forgive you," but even as I said these words my heart remained angry or resentful. I still wanted to hear the story that tells me that I was right after all; I still wanted to hear apologies and excuses; I still wanted the satisfaction of receiving some praise in return—if only the praise for being so forgiving.[47]

"Forgive us our trespasses as we forgive those who trespass against us" is not intended to place a condition upon our forgiveness, but acts as a believer's promise and description of the fruits of faith produced by a sanctified heart. "Forgive me, Lord, as I hereby have forgiven my boss, spouse, child, parent, etc." For "Who can discern all their errors?" (Ps 19:12). Yet non-verbal language is a powerful indicator of heartfelt feelings. God accepts it—so we ought to do likewise. "If you, O LORD, should mark iniquities, O Lord, who could stand?" (Ps 130:3). Besides, forgiving another person frees us to forgive all trespasses against us, liberating self from anger and resentment. For example, the bite of a poisonous snake is not the immediate cause of death. The victim's own lungs, which pump the venom throughout the rest of the body, are the real killer. So too, we are our worst enemy. A woman assaulted in a dark alley by a stranger and unable to eventually forgive her aggressor thereby prolongs his grip upon

---

47. Nouwen, *The Return of the Prodigal Son*, 129.

her conscience. His ghost persists as her unseen abuser until the day of her death. Instead of scars, open wounds persist and bleed. She is innocent. But the sin of another has made her impure.

Demons are regularly referred to as "unclean spirits." They love to share their impurities with us in their innovative manner of inciting us to hate and seek retaliation. They find their insidious foothold when we replay the abusive incident over and again in our minds through a paralyzing closed loop.[48] While frozen in a state of anger we gather the sins of those whom we have been commissioned to love into one large lump, justifying slandering with our stabbing lips or shunning them with our murdering hearts. St. Paul's therapy employs passive imperatives in the following loose paraphrase, "Let all bitterness and wrath and anger and clamor and slander be put away from you, along with all malice" (Eph 4:31). Without surrendering rage and hurt to Jesus, and eventually leaving all justice scales with the Lord, there is never any real closure. We continue to subjugate ourselves to abuse. The resultant guilt and shame is sure to unleash an acidic explosion on other innocent victims such as one's intimate entourage of friends, family and community. "Be angry and do not sin; do not let the sun go down on your anger, and give no opportunity to the devil" (Eph 4:26-27). Anger is normal and even honourable, reflecting an enigmatic love and passion for justice. Yet without eventual deliverance it has a bewildering tendency to lustfully multiply its objects and magnify the jealous scope of its fiery path. There were times that I resented Debby, angry at her spiritual "regression" and its repercussions for me. That being said, any abuse that I had suffered at the hand of Debby was incomparable with what she had undergone at the wicked hand of others. In each and every case, the sweetest words to a sinner's ears are "I forgive you all your sins" and "Take and eat, this is my body given for you."

+ + +

Despite all the skirmishes with spiritual oppression and possession, and in spite of any spoken tokens of apology a lot of the time, Debby would habitually insist upon buying me lunch at a local burger joint after each and every pastoral visit and spiritual siege. It was her peace offering. Though not a huge fan of fast food, I accepted the modest plunder. A different

---

48. Quoting Rev. Dr. John Kleinig during a lecture entitled *The Spiritual Disciplines* at Mount Carmel Retreat Center in Niagara Falls, Ontario, 2014.

parishioner who was demonically oppressed would prepare a lovely salad from her garden, and we would not speak about the dark battling that had transpired between us. It was symbolic. Mature Christians intuitively understand the reciprocal and mutually supportive relationship between laity and clergy. The pastor feeds the people the bread of heaven while the people provide for him the bread of the earth. They depend upon him for spiritual safety while he relies upon them for physical provisions. A healthy body harnesses the gifts of all of its members, while an unhealthy one seeks for them all in a select few. Even Debby had spiritual talents—however unobtrusive they were. Mostly she felt like a burden. Lord, forgive us.

Even pastors can be so heavenly-minded as to be of little earthly good when we judge others as inferior to ourselves. Instead of gracefully digging my shepherd heels into the earth—finding God and serving Him right there in the muck—I would have preferred tilting my haughty head upwards and fixing my "holier-than-thou" eyes towards the New Jerusalem. Yet heaven had indeed manifested itself on earth: Debby carried Christ in her heart, and into our midst, offering us a chance to serve *Him* through taking care of *her*. Unlike the "prince of the power of the air" (Eph 2:2), the King, Emmanuel, stoops down from heaven and remains incarnate, on earth: "God with us."

Debby tarried in an unalterable state of humiliation. Her personal successes were practically nonexistent. She was sick, overweight and had no form or majesty that one should look at her. She held no beauty that one should desire her. Joel Osteen would have run. Yet God found her beautiful. *She was victorious.* Sometimes, though, Debby would apologize for requiring too much of my time. I was often tempted to agree with her regrets, but then I would catch myself and instead explain to her that, had she not contacted me at her moment of crisis and shared with me her grief, I would have missed another opportunity to speak, not only *for* God, but *to* God; jettisoning a chance to tap into the fountain of an unending hymn, the *Sanctus*, being sung ceaselessly by the company of heaven to the Lamb on the eternal throne. It was *I* who was compelled to thank *her*. God places hurting people in our path to keep us praying. He gives us our enemies to teach us how to love. One with Christ, we are mediators and "gods" in our vicarious intercessions (Ps 82:6). Like the paralytic whom the men carried to Jesus, crippled people offer us a chance to come once again into our Lord's presence. The abundance of God's grace blesses both us and them, even when they are unaware (Luke 5:17–26).

Who's Afraid of the Steppenwolf?

As a military chaplain I always offer to pray for people after a counseling session or intervention. Most agree—some reluctantly—but the majority leave with moistened eyes. Even when I was serving in a French-speaking province and encumbered by the vocabulary of a language that I had far from mastered, choked-up soldiers would cleave to these personalized petitions. People aren't accustomed to hearing their names spoken before the sacerdotal courts of God. They thirst for Him. Jesus prays for them—through us. We are to pray without ceasing. In fact, we *do* pray without ceasing as the Holy Spirit, the Spirit of our Lord Jesus who has made us His temples, lets very few things impede Him from using us as His temples of prayer. The demons seek to hinder our journey with Jesus by attacking our prayer-life. The further one goes, the harder it gets. *Temptatio* follows *meditatio* like a fly on fruit. The telephone always seems to ring in those intense moments of prayer. Yet the Holy Spirit refuses to stop, unless we shut Him out of course. Mostly though, demonic efforts to distract our praying produce even godlier groans and ethereal moans as the Holy Spirit takes control. The loveliest music of prayer springs from crippled hearts. Incidentally, in this present battle Christians are wise to seek the company of their elders since soldiers learn the most from veterans. Broken, wounded, and sometimes still bleeding, their prayers offer a compelling model for our own.

It's not easy though. Focusing on something outside of oneself is never intuitive. For instance, when I pray, I find it to be an overwhelming challenge to reflect upon the nature of God for more than a moment. An ineffable chasm separates the divine from the human. We creatures can only guess at the divine nature, limited to conceptions of the almighty Creator's attributes in relation to ourselves. Therefore, much of our prayer life is innocently circumscribed by petitions instead of adorations. This is not selfish. But it does show how inadvertently speechless we are before One so entirely foreign to us. We attempt to understand Him within our limited frame of reference, requiring the use of anthropomorphisms or adjectival conceptualizations as the only way to describe divine attributes. The kind of meditation that occurs on Holy Trinity Sunday, where the relationship between the three distinct persons in the *homoousia*, or one essence, are the focus of our imaginative energies, offers a small window—no, a peephole—into the profound truth that there exists a fundamental gap between Creator and creature.

My First Exorcism

+ + +

I know now that prayer is a resting in the sunshine of grace, not a work of self, but an opening up to Christ. But when battling with the devil in Debby, I often obsessed intellectually as to why it all had to be so hard. I knew that Debby was a weak new convert, but why hadn't *my* prayers worked the first time? "Thy will be done." *The Small Catechism* taught that God's will is done when He breaks and hinders every evil plan and purpose of the devil. Doesn't the riddance of a demon clearly fall under that category? Did I lack adequate faith to get the job done right? Perhaps I employed the wrong words. Why did those demons keep returning to this helpless—albeit, *rebellious*, but still *helpless*—child of God? That was, I believe, the point. Unless our prayers spring forth from the barren fields of our hearts, they remain tangled in the roots of ego, wedged between the stumps of reason and strangled by the vines of self. In short, they remain *our* prayers. Instead, they must become *Christ's*.

Norwegian devotional writer Ole Hallesby once observed how helplessness indeed is the best friend of prayer[49] because that is the only way in which our petitions are handed over to God. My feeble prayers are perfect in every way as I stand in Christ's stead and He stands in mine. The eternal Father sees me, but He hears Jesus. Our prayers merge as one. Such a prayer must work. After all, it is perfectly conceivable that God would not listen to me, an enemy of His holiness. But His one and only Son—how could He not listen to Him? Debby was finally released—in His time, not mine. She died. Now she is free. Sometimes our prayers are reduced to tears, but those drops are precious, since they find their place in the tissue of Christ. He tucks it not away, but offers it up to His Father as His very own, dampened by His own tears; a cherished relic for the heavenly courts.

Spiritual war never centres in the power of our prayer, but rather the power of Christ. "My grace is sufficient for you, for my power is made perfect in weakness" (2 Cor 12:9). A heart permeated by misery and unable to poetically articulate a single petition produces a sweet-sounding canticle played from the lyre of Christ. Satan mobilizes all his forces to hinder such broken prayers. Completely contrary to typical military stratagem, this sly snake commandeers his troops to convince us, not that we are weak, but that we, in ourselves, are strong. Again, weakness alone forms the sole condition for a prayer prayed in Jesus' name. This is why all versions of

---

49. Hallesby, *Prayer*, 9.

a theology of glory are truly satanic. God accepts all that we despise and those whom we reject. Although we are prompted to think poorly of others in our hearts, the Saviour reminds us that the most uncomely parts of the body are indispensable; the least presentable, the most honorable (1 Cor 12:22–24). In the cavern of self-righteousness, the cross is our only cleft.

Prayers from a position of strength—"name it, claim it" and all other varieties that attempt to manipulate God into a gum-ball machine—are a demonic imitation of true prayer. Even when we get what we want, we are rarely better off. Yet even then, though the devil depletes, God gives. When our Lord takes away, He always gives more. With Debby, the lessons that I learned about grace, love, beauty and forgiveness surpass all worldly riches. They are treasures laid in heaven, where "neither moth nor rust destroys and where thieves do not break in and steal" (Matt 6:20). No wonder the deacon and martyr St. Laurence was adamant that the poor are the true treasures of the Church, as he underwent death on the gridiron by a greedy emperor searching for gold. The blood of all the martyrs, past and present, sows seed for the Church. Nothing evil escapes good use. God is too obsessed with our welfare for it to be otherwise: "grace upon grace" (John 1:16).

Oddly enough, although sin, strictly speaking, never proffers an occasion to celebrate, even it disguises a blessing: whenever a sinner repents, a myriad of angels rejoice (Luke 15:10). As one clergyman once observed, "the tears of penitent sinners are the wine and delicacies of the angels."[50] The devil weeps for other reasons as he is forced to fold his hand at each and every turn of the cosmological game.

> Bowed down beneath a load of sin,
> By Satan sorely pressed,
> By wars without and fears within,
> I come to Thee for rest.
>
> Be Thou my Shield and Hiding-place,
> That, sheltered near Thy side,
> I may my fierce Accuser face
> And tell him Thou hast died.[51]

---

50. Adams, *The Christian Treasury*, 240.
51. TLH 456.

The Lion, the Witch and the Lord's Supper

> Whoever makes a practice of sinning is of the devil, for the devil has been sinning from the beginning. The reason the Son of God appeared was to destroy the works of the devil. (1 John 3:8)

My mother shared with me a story of an old pastor at a German Lutheran church. He was attacked by a demoniac during the *Gottesdienst*. The ushers needed to restrain him and called the police. Apparently, he possessed the strength of many men. She had forgotten most of the details of the follow-up, other than it turned out that the individual had been reading occult books and spent the remainder of his life incarcerated in a mental institution.

Less dramatic, but equally significant, I recall a physical skirmish over the Lord's cup with an elderly woman who had approached the altar for a blessing in her baptismal grace. Because her church body was not in altar fellowship with our own, she was forbidden to partake of the consecrated elements. At first, she appreciated the historic practice of reserving the sacrament only for catechized members. But then, something changed her mind. She advanced towards the chancel in protest and insisted on communing. Despite my objection, she grabbed hold of the cup and snarled. The tug-of-war was easily overcome, but the event left me quite shaken. Indeed it was a worthwhile fight, as I knew that it would have been to her detriment, a clear "drinking judgment upon herself" as St. Paul warns (1 Cor 11:29). Like medicine offered to one to whom it is not prescribed, abuse of the holy Sacrament can lead to both spiritual and physical illness—even death (1 Cor 11:30).

Many members of my congregation expressed their indignation and disapproval at my decision. Unconvinced that my reaction was rooted

The Lion, the Witch and the Lord's Supper

in love, they assumed that her exclusion involved questions of her moral worthiness (sigh). "God welcomes all, pastor, hadn't you heard?" one elder smirked. Blinded by emotions and displaying no concern towards her confessional or doctrinal beliefs, they were convinced that the lady was believing, desperate and sincere—or so it appeared. Our world encourages us, after all, to follow our hearts—even when eclipsed by God's Word. "It's not Canadian to judge. It's just not polite." Yet there remains a fine line between politeness and apathy. No one actually believes in moral relativism, although it remains fashionable to expound the idea in social settings. Otherwise the exclamation, "I myself would never be a paedophile, but to each his own," wouldn't raise your blood pressure or churn your stomach. Deep down, all people believe that what is good for them is good for others. Although some judgments are driven by racism and hatred, others are driven by a sincere concern over a neighbour's well-being. Treating others as you would wish to be treated is the essence of love. Although people praise neutrality, God calls it "lukewarm," disdaining it for good reason. It is fear under the guise of political correctness—not love—that tempts us to say nothing.

A few Sundays later, a man who was unknown to the clergy staff approached the altar, but was also denied the Eucharist. Whether he was mentally ill or demonically oppressed was unclear. He made the sign of the holy cross in mocking jest while mumbling some unintelligible words in an effort to emulate the officiant. Uninterested in catechesis aimed at membership, it became apparent later that he only wished to cause strife and division within the body of Christ by attacking that very body of our Lord in its manifestation in the Holy Supper: an appropriate strategy indeed. Although demons detest the preaching of the glorious cross and private confession robs them of critical ammunition against both the demoniac and the exorcist, the Holy Eucharist poses the most devastating blow.

If you want to see a demon, you can be guaranteed a "sighting" during a Holy Communion service—but not necessarily with the naked eyes. The Lord's sacred meal is the zenith of demonic raid. It is the headquarters targeted by Satan's henchmen. In hate of the holy Eucharist demons seek to yank it into the realm of the profane. For in the pouring out of blood—from the cross, down the throats and into the souls of believing Christians—atonement has been made. The pagan gods of the underworld thirst for blood, a notion mimicked in occult rituals. Well, by this pool of cleansing blood they are drowned as in a pernicious and inescapable ocean. Their resurfacing heads are soaked by the constant flow of this liquid of life that finds its source in the Church's chalice. Though defeated at Calvary, these sore and bitter losers continue to wage war on Christ whom they find still enfleshed in the Lord's Supper. Satan does not care whether or not one is religious, has faith, or confesses that God is one, is almighty, and is sovereign. He believes the same, and shudders at the thought (Jas 2:19). Satan is not threatened by theocentric missionary endeavours and acute apologetics regarding the existence of God—until they lead to Christocentric dogma on Christ's apotheosis in the Holy Eucharist.

In spite of the menacing gargoyles poised on the ledges of some ancient churches symbolizing the presence of evil outside of their walls, the devil's chief target is something within: the body of Jesus. Naturally he finds Him in the chalice and paten as bread and wine are offered into the mouths of believers each and every Sunday. It is no wonder that a closed communion practice remains one of the most heated and divisive issues in the apostolic Church today. For churches that only strive to be user-friendly, welcoming and inclusive, withholding the consecrated elements from any professing Christian is *a tad* counterproductive. Yet what responsible parent doesn't lock the medicine cabinet at home when kids are around? What is medicine for one is poison to another. Coming to God isn't about feeling comfortable, but about being safe. As the Orthodox liturgy for St. James accurately summarizes: "Holy things for holy ones" as *the* Holy One enters through the portal of the divine liturgy.

At every mass the devil shivers. But he still manages to concentrate his unrelenting assaults on active faith in the purifying presence of Christ in the consecrated elements. In some Christian traditions, the worshipper genuflects at the words "He was made man" during the Nicene Creed, since these are some of the most horrifying words apprehended by demons during the Divine Service. The incarnation spelled their defeat. "Since therefore the children share in flesh and blood, he himself likewise partook of the same things, that through death he might destroy the one who has the power of death, that is, the devil" (Heb 2:14). How appropriate it was to worshipfully bow at the words before which the denizens of hell cower. Likewise, pastors continue to venerate the Host in elevation, as the *Agnus Dei* is sung in worship of the Christ who is once again enfleshed among us in, with and under bread and wine. A polluted belief regarding the Sacrament of the Altar, established on a depraved and demonic teaching of the same, compels the Church to carefully guard the true doctrine and provide

The Lion, the Witch and the Lord's Supper

her best efforts in articulating it clearly and concisely to the assembly of believers. For this reason, Holy Communion remains one of the greatest obstructions to conversion, and unity, in the Church. Needless to say, early Christians were regarded as cannibals—so clearly did they profess the presence of the true body and blood in the Sacrament—that they were executed for their beliefs. If history repeats itself, our future looks glum.

Many church bodies agree with the main menu of Christian teaching, but they have great difficulty swallowing this last bite. Jesus' words, "Unless you eat the flesh of the Son of Man and drink his blood, you have no life in you" (John 6:53) is a thorn in the side for many churches, and rightly so. St. Paul cautions that a lighthearted practice springing forth from false teaching makes one a participant with demons: "You cannot drink the cup of the Lord and the cup of demons. You cannot partake of the table of the Lord and the table of demons" (1 Cor 10:20–21). Typically, this rebuke has been one of the scriptural supports for altar fellowship amongst like-minded believers who share the same public confession. Communion fellowship is never *created* through Eucharistic participation. Instead, it is an *expression* of a pre-existing fellowship. When communion occurs, participants show forth that they are already of the same accord. To endorse communion fellowship as a means of creating artificial unity is not only unbiblical, but it is a dishonest and devilish trick on the uninformed laity. Bickering over this point does not betray "high theology" either. Jesus sets the priorities. When some Christians claim that clergy are "splitting hairs" over the "fine points" of doctrine (i.e. that which they consider to be irrelevant), I wonder whether or not they would apply the same casuistic standard to a doctor who is carefully viewing their x-rays or consulting the medical manuals before their surgery. After all, clearly, physical health makes for easier living. Spiritual health secured through a diet of solid doctrine makes for a more peaceful Christian journey, as each of the precious faithful ones are equipped by God in their crucial mission of influencing the world around them. This, however, is not intuitive. It is grasped by faith.

In seeking to avoid the issue, some laity sigh that these sorts of doctrinal matters are too daunting for their simple minds. However, these same self-proclaimed "simple folk" scrutinize their bills and tax records, demonstrating great competency in the fine details of study. The temptation to refrain from issues that we find unsettling falls under "laziness," included by Roman Catholics as one of their seven mortal sins. The main tenets of Christian theology are readily within the reach of every believer both young and old. God expects every Christian to be a theologian of a sort since "doing theology" is pure worship. Having no other gods and hallowing His name is none other than learning and receiving all that His holy name means for us. The *study of God* rests in stark contrast with a *study of man*, a comfortable and familiar focus on self.

For instance, sentimental praise songs, once the words have been carefully examined, do not usually glorify God, but make us feel better about ourselves—for one brief moment. Some of them do not even mention Jesus, never mind proclaiming the Gospel. Such worship acts as a drug that soothes the complacent Old Adam. It is alien to doxological confession of the majestic and praiseworthy identity of our Triune Lord. The devil would have us all exalt God to our neighbour (like the nine healed lepers who did not return to thank Christ) rather than have any one of us return to Jesus and enjoy true fellowship with Him in the Divine Service. Distracting believers from the Redeemer's real and corporal presence among us, even in a vigorous church filled with holy sounds and loving Christians, is a game about which the evil one is master. Holy Communion does, after all, represent his ruin. "Dear Christian guests, sing away to your almighty God and praise his holy name," the devious spirits slyly whisper, "as long as you do not attend His noxious feast!"

The Lord's Supper is a Christian's greatest source of comfort and hope on this side of eternity. The devil knows this better than we do, and so he assaults it from every possible position. One poignantly biblically literate and sincere seeker of scriptural truth was peculiarly plagued by demons. It turned out that she was an ex-cult member. Voices inside her head whispered to her that I, the pastor, was untrustworthy at the very moment that she had made contact with our church. The same disparaging voices would habitually reiterate to her that she was a disappointment to her family, that she would be better-off dead, and that she should make that happen herself immediately. Satan is, after all, not simply a liar but also a murderer (John 8:44). The only pillar of strength that buffeted her accusing conscience was Holy Communion. Prayer helped, and so did hearing the Word. But this dejected lamb longed for something tangible, and less immaterial. Encumbered by an unremitting self-commiseration for longer than she could remember, she required more than a letter from her loving Saviour, but needed an encounter with Him in person. She hungered and thirsted for grace. Since she was home-bound, I would carry the sacrament to her monthly. Between these celebrations, counsel was offered her over the telephone, for the provocative voices were persistent. In that church I think I spent more time on the phone offering private absolution and praying with people than I did in person. When the vociferous voices were too strong, my prayers consisted exclusively—even legalistically—of words of the Holy Scripture. I stayed clear of any interpolations of my own lest the voices accuse me of adding to the Word and casting further doubt on my ministry to her. Curiously, the singing of hymns seemed to help even though they expressed poetic and creative articulations of the Gospel that were not verbatim Scripture. Yet, in those moments when I would interject with my own reflections, she would lose control and begin to distrust. It wasn't personal. I was simply the steward. The gifts did not belong to me. They never do. I didn't mind—much.

+ + +

On still another fortuitous occasion, a fragile eccentric middle-aged woman, a former member of the Jehovah Witnesses, was attracted to our church after reading a statement of our beliefs and Confessions on our web page. She had explored various churches but without satisfaction. Though a believer in the real presence of our Lord in the consecrated bread and wine, she had never been permitted to receive it. In the Jehovah Witness services, the organization's version of the holy sacrament passes by each member during their worship service. Yet only those who believe themselves to be worthy enough are allowed to take and eat the bread. Consequently, only the most morally self-righteous and socially bold members of the assembly receive it, while the humble at heart and broken in spirit are denied access to God's forgiving presence. As to whether or not anything is actually offered in a supposed sacramental event officiated by a cult is doubtful. But that is beside the point. For those misguided believers, acceptance into the kingdom of God is based upon one's inherent worthiness. And any honest follower of Christ intuitively knows that he or she does not measure up to the divine standard. The communion services were moments of great sorrow for this spiritually wounded individual. She thirsted. She hungered. She hoped that one day she would be deemed fit to partake of this meal of grace. She described her bereavement when viewing the bread pass her by in terms of physical pain, like a series of sharp pins penetrating an already bleeding heart. As all the angels in heaven rejoice at each episode of repentance, it probably holds true that all the company of hell lauds such crushing of Christian faith. A river of tears splashed upon the altar rail the first time she received the Holy Eucharist at our church. The intensity of her joy fluctuated little in each subsequent celebration.

After her reception into membership, I was intrigued to hear snippets of her conversion story. In her younger years, she had believed on Jesus as the tender-hearted saviour after having been invited into the house of a stranger during her bi-weekly door to door witnessing campaigns. The typical recruitment dialogue had resulted in afternoon tea in the home of a Christian who had decided to play a record of Gospel-centred Scripture verses. At hearing the Good News that Christ had died for her and required nothing from her in return, she wept. The report that Jehovah had achieved everything necessary for salvation caused her both sorrow and grief over all the years of doubting His love paired by the deepest happiness that salvation was that easy. She had already been plucked into the hand of God, purchased and won by the costly and victorious efforts of her Saviour, and nothing could change that reality.

The majority of middle-class North Americans just assumes that God loves them. "Why wouldn't He, after all? Aren't we loveable?" Most of us, on occasion, have been eulogized for our goodness and we effortlessly agree with that crowd-pleasing assessment. But for someone who had maintained an accurate picture of her maimed status before God—evaluated according to His terms and not her own—such presuppositions were unfounded. "No one is good except God alone" (Luke 18:19). This Jehovah's Witness understood that harsh truth, which is why she spent her life dedicated to improving her spiritual state with the slight hope that perhaps God would have mercy on her on Judgment Day. But hearing that God had *already* purged away all her sins, binding her heart and mind to His, making her completely worthy to be His child by the merits, kindness and righteousness of Christ earned for her at the cross and distributed to her through faith alone, was beyond her most imaginative expectations. With a unified voice the Church on earth pleads, "Yes, Lord, yet even the dogs eat the crumbs that fall from their master's table" (Matt 15:27). Those who ask for crumbs receive loaves—their demons take flight as well (Matt 15:28).

Lamentably, as a young and insecure woman whose husband was a respected leader within the organization, she did not possess the courage to officially abandon the sect immediately. Secretly, she believed in the true Faith, until finally one day, by the grace and strength of God, the two of them quit the institution formally, together. Although I welcomed them into their new spiritual home, I was unprepared for the immense amount of devilish baggage that accompanied them. This was not, by any means, their fault. But the immersion into a cultish worldview for decades naturally posed profound challenges in their adjustment to a new normalcy. For example, the first obstacle proved to be the crucifix. In accordance with their former beliefs, they held that any engraved image of our Saviour was an idol. Naturally, because the Holy Scriptures teach that Christ is the "exact representation" and "icon" of the invisible God (Col 1:15) all representations or depictions of Him are offensive to the enemy. The demons recoil at every image of the *Agnus Dei*, crucifix and sign of the holy cross. These ex-cultists' disturbance was amplified by the role that the crucifix played in the worshipping congregation: centred in the middle of the altar. It appeared as if people were praying to a metallic statue. To prove them wrong, our church reluctantly agreed to move the crucifix to the side of the chancel in order to demonstrate that the item was not as central to our worship as it may have seemed. Instead, it was a helpful reminder of God's saving grace and Christ crucified in our midst.

Now the reason I say "reluctantly" is that some felt that a stumbling block for one person was insufficient reason to omit something that elevates the happiness of the rest, even temporarily. The parable of the Lord's search for the one lost sheep at the expense of the ninety-nine quickly eradicated that argument in a debate that took the better half of the afternoon. However fatiguing, every church conflict ought to be embraced with relief and not disdained. The congregation under attack is a church over which the devil finds it worth fighting. Pastors can derive the sweetest of consolations from those moments when the wicked one meddles in ways intended to cast them into despair. Spiritual attack is proof of God's presence and vocational integrity. When the devil gives us turmoil, we are convinced that we are saved. To quote one expert in the field of exorcism, "The worst temptation is no temptation."[1] Rejoice, therefore, when you are assaulted.

The one day in the Church calendar that highlights spiritual warfare is St. Michael and All Angels. The reading from *The Revelation to St. John* describes the great dragon Lucifer as "filled with fury because he knows that his time is short" (Rev 12:12). Outsmarted and beaten, he is unable to devour the royal-blooded newborn baby who has been snatched up to heaven. With untamed vengeance, this thwarted limping beast chases after

---

1. Quoting John Kleinig during a lecture entitled *The Spiritual Disciplines* at Mount Carmel Retreat Center in Niagara Falls, Ontario, 2014.

His mother who is the Church on earth. Apocalyptic literature does not foretell the future as much as it forecasts the events of the present which are draped in the hidden realms of a cosmic battle. The devil and his demons have been evicted from the kingly court and defeated by the death, resurrection and ascension of the Prince of heaven. These sore losers seek revenge. Obviously they leave their friends alone and only attack those by whom they feel themselves threatened. Because "there must be factions" (1 Cor 11:19) it is the happy churches that should be afraid. The peaceful congregation is suspect. The disciples who follow Jesus to Jerusalem while He prophesies His death rightly fear, even though there is no doubt that they are treading the right path (Mark 10:32).

My wife is probably tired of hearing my frustrating rants about being praised for a good sermon by non-practicing Christians, since, according to my line of reasoning, the unrepentant and unbelievers should have found more by which to be offended. The Gospel is robbed of its joy when the Law has not been preached in all its heaviness and fury. Moments of suffering and distress are key places in which God's hidden glory and bounteous grace are revealed. The onsets of Satan are evidence of our Lord's presence. "If it is by the Spirit of God that I cast our demons, then the kingdom of God has come upon you" (Matt 12:28).

+ + +

Eventually, most of our church council was convinced that helping to remove a perceived stumbling block for the sake of a brother or sister in the Lord (in this case ex-Jehovah Witnesses) was a worthwhile endeavour, even if most of them were unable to conceive how a believer could take such offence at a representation of Jesus. Pastors are always advised to "not be overcome by evil, but overcome evil with good" (Rom 12:21). Lutheran American Army chaplain Henry Gerecke was appointed to provide spiritual care to the Nazi war criminals sentenced to death at the Nuremberg trials. He asked God to preserve him from all pride and prejudice as he battled "for the souls of men standing beneath the shadows of the gallows."[2] Miraculously, one received Holy Communion hours before his death confessing with tears, "You have helped me more than you know. May Christ, my Saviour, stand by me all the way. I shall need him much."[3]

---

2. Townsend, *Mission at Nuremberg*, 8.
3. Ibid 11.

The Lion, the Witch and the Lord's Supper

He was not the only convert either.[4] God's mercy is incredibly powerful and His grace abundant (Rom 5:17). I, too, remarked that, while trying to persuade some stubborn Eastern European businessmen to accommodate an, albeit, unreasonable request. Besides teaching us how to love those different from ourselves, the discussion regarding the issue of images proved to be a fruitful activity in theological reasoning as well. Thinking usually is. Postmodernists, Roland Barthes and Jacques Derrida, suggest that dialogue is redundant unless a new perspective is shared, one which opens up a new communicative horizon. In other words, when two people agree, one of them is unnecessary. Some blithesome pastors are allergic to doctrinal debate and shy away from exploring the extra-linguistic reality underlying most theological discussions rather than embracing these opportunities as methods of sharpening their own reasoning tools. With regards to the crucifix, removing the figure from its central location was a clear indication that either we were worshipping an invisible God, or that we were paying homage to a brick wall—or perhaps the cars in the parking lot on the other side. In fact, worship should be conducted in prayer with eyes closed. Scripturally based liturgies ought to be memorized in all of their repetitions. The liturgy is, after all, an intimate and heart-felt conversation between God and His Bride (and conversations are most sincere when they are spoken and not read). Images and pictures in the Church help redirect our eyes to that which is unseen when our eyes are open. Christians do not require images to worship, though they are a great help. Instead we worship nothing other than the unseen God. Christians see with their eyes closed.

A further compelling argument stemmed from the undeniable phenomenon that every religious human being makes some sort of image of God in their mind's eye, informed by their upbringing and cultural particularities. We may as well have an accurate portrayal before our faces to best inform the inevitable images created by our thoughts. On the other hand, although Jesus was historically Jewish, the best pictures of our Lord should look the least like any historic individual that we have encountered on the street. Though we have all seen various ethnic expressions of Jesus, the ambiguous images (not to be confused with androgynous ones!) are more effective indicators of the universal human nature, which He assumed by the virgin birth. Our new catechumen's arguments against representations of the Divine were by no means foolish, I dare say. Indeed, they had all been wisely resolved in the early ecumenical councils of the Church shortly after

---

4. Ibid 277.

the legalization of the Christian Church. Yet the decisions were preceded by years of heated and intense discussion based on Biblical hermeneutics and exegesis. The Old Testament prohibition of making graven images of an invisible God could not be ignored. The most remarkable insight was that since the incarnation, people now knew, at least in part, what God looked like. He looked like us! We may not be privy to all the exact details regarding hair length, eye colour, and stature. But we do know that Jesus was a Jewish man who hung on a cross with a crown on His head.

The incarnation was an assumption of the world into the life of God—the radical means for providing humankind safe access to His glory. Our dazzling God had become ordinary flesh, a flesh common to all people of all races of both sexes. The Word had become flesh; the invisible appeared in visible form. A crucifix simply re-presented this emphatic truth. It is not intended as an image for worship. It is a sermon—a visible Word and preaching of the Gospel. Accordingly, the Orthodox consider icons as *written* not painted.[5] "I would have you know nothing but Christ crucified," broadcasts St. Paul (1 Cor 2:2). Albeit, none of this was tolerated in the Old Testament as God clearly forbade man-made creations of His likeness. At the same time, He had provided for worship specific instructions to His people for the design of images on the curtain in the temple and the sculptured golden cherubim adorning the Ark of the Covenant. The distinguishing difference was that He Himself had provided and mandated the images. So too, with the Christ event through the virgin birth God Himself had provided the image, rendering many of those Old Testament restrictions obsolete. After all, "no one puts new wine into old wineskins. If he does, the new wine will burst the skins and it will be spilled, and the skins will be destroyed." (Luke 5:37).

+ + +

Finally, through a series of Bible studies and prayer, this former Jehovah Witness was persuaded by the Gospel. But she still had some doubts. Who doesn't? "Have mercy upon us, O Lord" (Ps 123:3).

---

5. Lutheran dogmatician, Francis Pieper concurs with this notion in his understanding of the Gospel as a means of grace expressed, not only through text and oral proclamations, but also through visual forms such as crucifixes and paintings, all of which demonstrate the remarkable compassion of God who makes His salvation readily and easily available. See Pieper, *Christian Dogmatics vol. III*, 106.

The Lion, the Witch and the Lord's Supper

Rise! To arms! With prayer employ you,
O Christians, lest the foe destroy you;
For Satan has designed your fall.
Wield God's Word, the weapon glorious;
Against all foes be thus victorious,
For God protects you from them all.
Fear not the hordes of hell, Here is Emmanuel.
Hail the Saviour! The strong foes yield to Christ, our shield,
And we, the victors, hold the field.[6]

---

6. LSB 668.

The World According to *der Zeitgeist*

> Now the Spirit expressly says that in later times some will depart from the faith by devoting themselves to deceitful spirits and teachings of demons. (1 Tim 4:1)

The ex-cultist's mild expostulation was admirable despite its lack of a solid Biblical foundation. It is a healthy sign when Christians engage themselves in theological debate as it reveals their concern for the important things in life. Etymologically, theology means "study of God." Again, the kind of Christian who proudly claims to care little about theology is usually clueless with regards to the foolishness of their opinion and mental sloth, even when they formally adhere to orthodox beliefs. Every Christian should, therefore, seek to sharpen his or her theological reasoning skills. There are few more wholesome forms of worship than talking about God. Clergy are called to "rightly handle the word of truth" (2 Tim 2:15). A pastor "must hold firm to the trustworthy word as taught, so that he may be able to give instruction in sound doctrine and also to rebuke those who contradict it" (Titus 1:9). To the disappointment of many zealous Christians, nothing is mentioned regarding building programs for church growth, strategies for advancing a social Gospel, inventories of felt-needs or even fostering a warm spirit of collective identity.

Doctrinal subjects are often tragically undervalued. It is a disturbing sign of our times that most churches care little about theological issues while negating creedal differences as "trifle," indicative of a survivalist mentality that seeks to merge forces with sectarian bodies in light of decreasing congregational membership. Many within the Emerging Church present Christianity as one big elephant to be explored and extolled in various

The World According to *der Zeitgeist*

ways: blindfolded believers describe their subjective experiences with Christ through their respective churches differently from their neighbours because they happen to touch a different part of the whole. But whether the leg, tail or head, they encounter the same praiseworthy creature. The Hindus neglected to copyright the analogy three thousand years ago.

In essence, it doesn't matter how you worship, as long as you are sincere. *You* may prefer the liturgical model, while *I* prefer to connect with God through adapting rock lyrics that compare God's love with ice cream. Never mind that the road to hell is paved with good intentions. It seems to me that God had a fairly precise methodology as to how He wanted to be worshipped (i.e. how He sought to serve us)—just ask Nadab and Abihu! (Lev 10:1–2)—and this was carefully carried into the New Testament era. A surgeon takes great care in the placement of his instruments in the ICU, even if the patient may lack a comprehension as to the logic that underlies those choices. "You seem rather rigid," the modern ecumenist argues, "Don't you believe in celebrating what we have in common? Didn't Christ pray that we all be one?" In light of the increasingly splintered denominational landscape that surrounds us, every believer should weep over disunity, especially when it occurs over the issues of culture, language and historical accident. But how ought we to treat all the crucial theological matter that we *do not* have in common? The devil is in the details. "A little leaven leavens the whole lump" (1 Cor 5:6).

In the early Church, ardent struggles were fought over what, today, would be deemed as minor differences in Christology. The Bible warns the Church against such apparent wisdom that does not descend from above, but is "earthly, unspiritual, demonic" (Jas 3:15). It does not take a lot of poison to kill a child. False doctrines are the poison to a soul seeking spiritual nourishment. Certainly some are more venomous than others. But they are all hazardous. Some make you sick, while others may kill. The Samaritans were characterized as having demons, not because of something that they did, but because of who they were: a *religious* sect broken away from mainline Judaism (John 8:48). Jesus rebukes Peter as "Satan," not because of something that he *does*, but because of what he *says*. Accordingly, in the Bible the perpetuation of false doctrine is likened to the parasitic spread of gangrene (2 Tim 2:17), a snare of the devil from which one's only escape is through a radical return to good teaching (2 Tim 2:24–26). Because of their implications for eternity, false teachings are more horrendous than the most grotesque torturous instruments of Hussein or Pinochet; more dangerous than the most heinous crimes against humanity. False doctrine can be likened to a hairpin crack in an airplane, which, if located in just the right spot, can bring the whole vehicle down in a crash. In 2000, a Singapore Airlines flight cost the lives of 183 passengers due to a single, innocent human error. By confusing two runways, one under construction repair, the pilot made the wrong turn upon take off. Fatal consequences stem from false information.

A story in WWII recalls soldiers being misled over enemy lines because they had been mistakenly outfitted with wrong coordinates for a meeting place. The numbers were off by only one single digit. Nevertheless, it resulted in their capture as prisoners of war. Accordingly, a habit of dogmatic astuteness is methodologically displayed in the military's attention to detail. All military discipline is intended to preserve lives. During room inspection in basic training, the placement of one soldier's gear is expected to look exactly identical to all the rest. If you were severely injured in a battle and your fellow soldier was unable to successfully locate your tourniquet because it was not located in the exact same place as your neighbour, the time lapse could cost you your life. We are spiritual warriors. Chaos theory declares that tiny changes have momentous effects. Precision saves lives. Theological precision is underestimated. Nonetheless, it achieves the same vital effect. It is lamentable, but true, that a faulty view of God leads to despair or turns people into self-righteous egoists, planting their feet in hell unaware. But it can also turn them into religious terrorists and suicide bombers: "A time is coming when they will kill you thinking they are offering service to God" (John 16:2). They are devil worshippers, however unknowingly. A quote traditionally attributed to Martin Luther reads:

> If I profess with the loudest voice and clearest exposition every portion of the truth of God except precisely that little point which the world and the devil are at that moment attacking, I am not confessing Christ, however boldly I may be professing Christ.[1]

The Church is mandated to prudently handle matters of doctrine. It is noteworthy that not murder, theft, nor abuses of various kinds pose the greatest threats to the safety of humankind. Instead, apostasy manifests the most terrorizing form of demonic confusion. Even common wars are the result of false teachings. Salman Rushdie once mused how fundamentalism is not about religion, but about power. Regardless, knowledge is power, and the Taliban recognize that an educated population is their most pestilent

---

1. Smith, *The Life and Letters of Martin Luther*, 324.

threat, while schools such as the *Madrasa* remain their most effective weapon. Teaching matters because information changes people. The world was created by a series of words, as is faith. Even secular belief-systems are underpinned by ideas about God and faith. Heresies are the untrue versions. While not all wars are caused by religion—a ridiculous assertion indeed—some are. But even those that aren't are usually still driven by misplaced convictions and misconstrued beliefs: honour is valued over forgiveness, justice over mercy, etc.

This world will come to an end. Yet spiritual combat has eternal repercussions. Demonic activity penetrates both. The demons are, thus, accurately labelled as "deceitful spirits" who engage in false teachings as their most destructive weapon (1 Tim 4:1). The evil one attempted to use the holy Word against Jesus during His temptations in the wilderness. We can be assured that he will resort to the same tactics with us. Soldiers fighting *Al Qaeda* discontinued the disposing of electronic waste in common trash bins after discovering that the terrorist weaponry was ingeniously assembled with bits and pieces of their own scrapped gear. Even virtually dead cell phone batteries and bits of damaged wiring were rigged into lethal land mines. The devil usurps another man's tools and uses them against him. He does this with the Truth. The Lord Jesus equates lying with murder, calling Satan "a murderer from the beginning" who "does not stand in the truth, because there is no truth in him. When he lies, he speaks out of his own character, for he is a liar and the father of lies" (John 8:44). False teaching robs the faithful believer of the spiritual medicine necessary for eternal salvation. Blasphemy corrupts that which is exclusively accessed in the name and teachings about the one true God. All the evils of our physical condition are short-lived. Yet our spirits continue forever, which is why one lost soul outweighs all the evils of the earth throughout all time and places. In other words, one eternal thing is worth more than all temporal things combined. And yet, in a spirit of sincere ecumenism, practically all mainline churches have begun to confess in syncretistic union a new ecumenical creed that says, "Let's get over silly trite items of pedantic doctrine and unify ourselves on whatever else is left." Certainly, it is a pragmatic and more cost-effective solution than maintaining two Christian churches of apparently similar confessions across the street from each other.

But Christianity has never made sense to humankind. It is foolishness and a stumbling block to the unbelieving world. True unity is reserved for heaven. When the pragmatist Judas Iscariot criticizes the prostitute's act of worship in anointing her Lord's feet with expensive perfume, Jesus promises that the poor will remain with us forever. The Lord's kingdom is not of this world despite all attempts at actualizing it on earth. Throughout most of its history, the Church understood her *raison d'être as* the preserver of the invariable Truth foundational to salvation. There were no small points of doctrine. Back then, no one contested that divergence from the one true Faith through acts of syncretistic fellowship between bodies of differing doctrinal confessions would result in lost membership in the heavenly kingdom. Today, it is encouraged. Nevertheless, the Church's mandate has not changed. One wonders as to whether or not the judgments that we are required to make on earth will extend into the afterlife, when we will even judge angels and demons (1 Cor 6:3) and crush Satan under our feet.

Surely, what is labelled "dogmatic snobbery" will not make faithful churches any more popular in the world or within Christendom. When deciding whether or not to stay in Narnia, the newly-converted Susan, hungry and cold from her treacherous journey confesses, "I wonder if there is any point of going on. . .I mean, it doesn't seem particularly safe here and it looks as if it won't be much fun either."[2] Christianity is neither safe nor fun. But it is worth the trek. Biblical worship and confessional integrity are increasingly unattractive and dangerous considering the trajectory of Christendom's evolution. Despite the popular opinions emanating from today's ecumenical climate, Reformation churches are best to underscore their differences instead of their commonalities if they really want to make a difference and change the world.[3]

We can only achieve this goal when we firmly believe with the early Church and apostles that no deviation from God's Word, no matter how seemingly small, is insignificant. The *Book of Revelation* uses the number 666 as a symbol for the devil because it is only one short of 777, a number that represents the perfectly holy Triune God. The devil is a fake and an imposter. He is the antithesis of beauty, but is a good pretender. For God, holiness is not calculated by degree. Before God, *coram Deo*, one is either holy or unholy. This is the most blessed relief for a Christian who doubts the certainty of his or her salvation: that—in spite of all appearances and

---

2. Lewis, *The Lion, the Witch and the Wardrobe*, 57.

3. In today's pluralistic landscape, the general consensus is that we learn more from our differences than we do from our commonalities—at least in theory. Unfortunately, most inter-faith discussion led by Western facilitators deeply fear expressions of real philosophical difference, revealing their own insecurities, uneasiness in becoming truly vulnerable, and preoccupation with controlling the dialogue.

experiences to the contrary—God has declared and made him or her impeccably holy due to the merits of Christ. After all, falling short of His glory by even a tad creates an infinitely wide chasm between us and Him. Again, the mark of the beast is not a 0, but rather a thrice 6. It is a marginal gap, but makes a world of difference. Yet it is precisely within that tiny fissure that the devil seeks to imitate his Creator and "ape" God.[4] Lacking originality, this skilled plagiarist's mockery captivates unguarded masses. False doctrine is nothing other than corrupted true doctrine. The ideal is crippled. It is distorted and bent out of its perfect shape. For the astute theologian, it is often an obvious and silly imitation. But for the defenceless one who has never fully laid eyes on the object being imitated, it can be a convincing alternative. Genetically modified organisms are never better than the real thing. But any distinction is futile for those who have never digested real wheat. How often has the pastor heard the comment, "The two churches *look* practically the same," implying that they are. True peace cannot be founded on artificial expressions of confessional unity. In 1817 Frederick William III employed the Prussian Union between the Reformed and Lutheran churches, since the differences *appeared* miniscule. The political decision resulted in the spiritual demise of both.

If Jesus is called the Way and the Truth (John 14:6) congregations that err in matters of doctrine lie with the devil (John 8:44) and, hence, belong to the "synagogue of Satan" (Rev 3:9). Well-intended pastors and congregations who love the Lord but do not entirely abide by His Word may walk alongside the Antichrist without ever even realizing it (Matt 24:24). In other words, evil is not always obvious. It cannot be overstated that evil is not a thing in and of itself. Although the Manicheans may protest, evil is not the positive name of a created substance, but is the negative description of something perverted. The devil can only ape the truth, since he is unable to create: "You son of the devil, you enemy of all righteousness, full of all deceit and villainy, will you not stop making crooked the straight paths of the Lord?" (Acts 13:10) Predictably, witchcraft lacks originality. Instead of praying for enemies, spells are cast. The rituals of the satanic priesthood include mock baptisms, culminating in the black mass. In the twelve steps of a satanic pact, abjuring faith in the Eucharist and profaning the host by reserving particles for the black mass are an essential condition.[5] Blasphemies

---

4. AE 41:167.
5. Amorth, *More Stories*, 141.

against the Holy Spirit replace the orthodox creeds.[6] Subscribing to the devil with one's own blood connotes a transfer of spiritual allegiance and is especially effective.[7] Even the vicarious satisfaction finds its antithesis in voodoo and other sorts of spiritism, but instead of the gracious exchange of sin for blessing through the death of the holy Saviour, curses are transferred through common items. Some spells call for the burial of a toad that at the moment of suffocation draws with it the life of the particular human named in the sorcerer's curse. Magic words mock the divine Word with pacts that mimic holy covenants.[8] Lucifer is not a creator, since there is only one Maker, despite all his creative efforts in his manipulation of the good. In the Holy Scriptures, the false teachers and devil are portrayed as a sort of "tag team," who are in the end destroyed together: "And the devil who had deceived them was thrown into the lake of fire and sulfur where the beast and the false prophet were, and they will be tormented day and night forever and ever" (Rev 20:10). We are wise to think likewise.

I once served an emotionally depressed woman who struggled with suicidal tendencies. Demeaning voices in her mind would incessantly chant that she was worth nothing, and that she may as well end her life instead of prolonging a hopeless version that dumped mountains of misery on her burdened but all too polite friends. Lies are nothing, but they still carry weight. In fact, the most effective lies are the subtlest distortions of the truth. They warp our perceptions. In all likelihood, the deluded woman's friends naturally found her condition to be a toilsome burden, but for most of them, that did not change their common love and concern for her. The devil's logic steers its victims down a deplorably deceptive route that always ends in death. It can be a convincing game, as the devil plays with half-truths. Most of us are not so gullible as to believe something entirely untrue, and considering that he is not a creator, the development of something truly untrue is inconceivable.

Apparently, the suicidal woman had overheard one of her friends complaining about how draining their one-sided friendship had been. In addition, she was persuaded from a selective and unbalanced reading of

---

6. Even in regular society we detect traces of evil blasphemy since the most effective cuss words are the ones that curse holy things and divine names.

7. Koch 138.

8. Incidentally, the magic words of fairy tales "hocus pocus" and "abracadabra" are likely derived from Christian vocabulary (e.g. the Latin Words of Consecration spoken during the Christian Mass and the name of the Holy Trinity) and were historically used by practitioners of the occult and witchcraft.

the Bible that, because of her sin and lack of spiritual progress, she had no worth to God and could not be saved. The Holy Scriptures can be used for our detriment. Using God's very own Word, the devil orchestrated some convincing arguments in his temptations of Christ in the desert. What the degrading and tantalizing voices did *not* tell her, was that she had been made worthy by the redemptive righteousness of Christ, given to her by grace in her baptism; that God loved her to the point of sacrificing His life on her behalf; and that *that* opinion, from *that* friend, counted more.

As a chaplain, I have lost track of the number of times I have advised governmental personnel against basing their personal value on evaluations from their supervisors. The opinions of other more significant people in one's life should trump the unfounded negative evaluations in the workplace. A social worker once shared how a greatly disheartened client of hers thought so lowly of himself, convinced that no one at all loved him, that in his suicide schematic he was determined to slice his throat with a plastic bag over his head in order to minimize any mess. With great consideration this thoughtful gentleman didn't want to inconvenience someone else in the cleanup! He did not want anyone to bother about him. Now there are various reasons for suicides. There are halfhearted suicide attempts that occur because people love themselves too much, for "no one ever hated his own flesh" (Eph 5:29a). If they actually hated themselves, they would want their earthly misery and pain to be extended, if you understand what I mean. Judas may fit into this category. But others are truly rooted in despair; those who think that they could never have any worth to anybody.

It is true that God owes us nothing. By nature we are unworthy, sinful and unclean. Yet the Great Shepherd *has* chosen to give us everything needful. The Aaronic benediction proclaimed at the end of the Divine Service joyfully reiterates that blessed promise. He makes His face shine upon us and is gracious to us. He looks upon us with favour and gives us peace. That God now sees us as worthy based on the vicarious satisfaction of Christ our Lord, is the part that the devil hides from us in our depression. His same half-truth strategy gained him victory in the Garden of Eden when he persuasively preached to our primordial forefathers, "You will be like God, knowing the difference between good and evil." Indeed, they knew no evil yet because they were, in fact, good. One mouthful of the fruit would, however, give them that sought-after knowledge, and a greater swig than they were prepared to swallow—an overdose that would consume them entirely.

In the Biblical age, blindness was interpreted as the worst form of divine punishment (John 9). In order to help them *feel physically* of what they were unaware spiritually (i.e. the dark state of their hearts), Elymas the Magician and Saul on the road to Damascus were both made blind (Acts 13:11; Acts 9:8). For Christians, spiritual blindness is primarily related to our hearing. God's unadulterated Word gives us sight. When Jesus is accused of working for the devil, others respond, "These are not the words of one who is oppressed by a demon. Can a demon open the eyes of the blind?" (John 10:21). Some rites for Holy baptism include the opening of the ears and mouth: "The Lord made the deaf hear and the dumb speak. Therefore in His name I say: Be opened, so that you may hear and speak the Word of God." So too, the downcast disciples recognized Jesus on the road to Emmaus only after He broke bread with them. Even though they should have perceived Him in hearing His teaching for the day, they were deaf. Yet God is merciful. He recalls to their memory the feeding of the five thousand or perhaps to an even more recent story of a "Last Supper."[9] So too, when we are deafened to His voice, we still recognize Him in the breaking of the bread in our Lord's Supper. Johann Heermaan writes in the hymn *O Christ, our true and only light*: "Fill with the radiance of thy grace the souls now lost in errors maze; enlighten those whose inmost minds some dark delusion haunts and blinds."[10] Christ has already navigated the labyrinth of hell. Hades, after all, has its microcosmic correspondence in the maze of our mind and soul. The Son of God knows them all thoroughly, and not only as an observer viewing our suffering planet from on high. He has become one of us to explore it Himself, with us, and for us, offering a way of escape. He is, and remains, man.

False teachings ultimately corrupt the good news that our kindhearted and loving God has saved us through faith. In catechesis, I have often explained to new members that being Lutheran amounts to consistently believing in being justified freely by grace alone. If one could paint a picture of the Gospel as the most beautiful rose imaginable, each of the delicate petals can be compared to church practices and dogmas. That innocent flower becomes incomplete and far less lovely when a petal falls away, or reveals traces of nibbling insects and other parasites. The worm that never

---

9. The relationship between Christ's death, supper and feeding of the masses may be best summarized poetically by Thomas Aquinas: "Though like the pelican to feed her brood, didst pierce Thyself to give us living food." LSB 640.

10. LSB 839.

dies (Mark 9:48) has a tendency to spread its pestilence to the adjoining petals. It is only a matter of time before only a stem remains, and all is lost.

Martyrdom, no matter how "grey," still hurts. They say that "Sticks and stones may break my bones but words will never hurt me." It is, however, untrue. Words are powerful. The Word became flesh and dwelt among us. Lies not only affect a healthy sense of self-esteem (when we are esteemed by Christ, that is), but will eventually rob us of our imperishable promised possession while ushering us down the wide and popular roads to the false and fiery gates. Believing untrue words not only temporarily alter the ways that we live, they recreate the reality in which we dwell—or at least our perception of it. I have witnessed in certain underdeveloped countries where paedophilia is tolerated or even socially sanctioned, a tendency for young children to become what they are not by nature or design. They transform into the persons that their abusers have sketched them to be. Likewise, a toxic work environment thrives where subordinates are micro-managed or undervalued. Instead of living up to higher expectations employees will often "live down" to lower ones. They end up behaving in accordance with the ways in which they are treated. There is a deep kernel of truth in Descartes' axiom: "I think therefore I am." We can easily become what others perceive us to be, or what we believe about ourselves. In the case of God, this can be good news. We are baptized. We are royal saints. Unfortunately His opinion often counts least.

+ + +

Demons are masters at confusing identities, both theirs and ours. In our present age, the trendiest dialogues circulate around questions of identity and sex. Our society's openly public discourses on the subject may be unique, but our obsession with the topic is not original. Other societies have proven more reverent in broaching the subject, recognizing, intuitively, that it is underpinned by something sacred. Yet even chivalrous norms cannot deride the uncanny percentage of the thoughts of the adult male population—in all times and places—from being consumed by content of a sexual orientation. It is a fetish of the rebellious nature. "Sins against the body" (1 Cor 6:18) are somehow different from all others. The body is a temple of the Holy Spirit (1 Cor 6:19), and, thus, sins of a sexual nature are of a particular offence. After all, heterosexual marriage and faithfulness within the divine institution of marriage is typological of Christ's mystical relationship with the Church. The dragon of hell pursues Christ's bride and employs every innovative means of perverting marital unions deemed sacred by God, until the day that he is swallowed up by the earth (Rev 12:13–16).

The devil may believe better than we that there is something profoundly sacramental about sexual union indicated by the perspicacious Biblical language of "becoming one flesh" (Gen 2:24). The God-man took on human flesh, purified it, and shares it with us for the life of the world in Holy Communion. Although mostly every generation obsesses over sex, there is a dignity to those societies that have tried to carefully handle the subject. The Victorian age was renowned for its cultural norms and etiquette, which courteously veiled the topic in English society. But, today, in the West, democratic man is embarrassed by the mystical, insulted by mysteries, and rejects honour in his pursuit of personal pleasure and instant gratification. For God, sex borders on the sacred and involves service. For man, sex is power.

In our post-modern age, being denied access to information is equated with authoritarianism and necessarily represents abuse of power by someone, somewhere. When Christians are rightly denied the Lord's Supper due to lack of instruction in the teachings and confessions of the church from which they seek it, their defenders judge the decision as legalistic, bureaucratic and even Kafkaesque. Fault-finders of church discipline reproach pastoral discretion as irrational and lacking common sense, discarding exegetical explanations as irrelevant. All formerly sacred subjects are open for dispute. The demonic handling of such topics is exemplified in the tiring dialogue over gender versus sex, in both university and popular media. One is "regretfully" born with a sex. But now, through generous government subsidies and a scientific community eager to explore the possibility of biological metamorphosis in mammals, one can "thankfully" choose his or her gender. Marriage has been redefined in terms of contractual consensus between two autonomous individuals. For Christians, this clash between reason and the divine Word amounts to absolute anthropological and ontological confusion over the nature of being male and female: two fundamentally different, but equally beautiful, ways of existing as human beings.

Secular society's present epidemic orbits around a nucleus of identity issues in collision with one another. On the one hand, trends in sexuality refuse to appeal to nature as the standard of normalcy. Mary Shelley's monster, *Frankenstein*, dramatically outlines the consequences of usurping a mandate that belongs to God alone by undertaking the manipulation of human nature through scientific alteration. On the other hand, examples from nature, such as hermaphroditic fish and plants are often employed as arguments for the 'naturalness' of transgender. Yet even if the argument is compelling, and people are born with atypical sexual tendencies, nature is an unreliable source for truth. The postlapsarian state of the world is permeated by a sinful nature, perverted and handicapped in its entire vicissitudes. The diversity of male and female is a lovely quality of creation crowned in the institution of marriage. Instead of viewing the unique roles pertaining to motherhood and fatherhood as a celebratory expression of diversity, societal elites interpret it as an unequal balance of power. The idea is manifested to a lesser extent in the controversial question of the ordination of women where phenomena originating in the kingdom of the Left are indiscriminately imported into the kingdom of the Right, confusing the two.[11] A single-vision hermeneutic lens, one that collapses theological distinctions between Law and Gospel, clergy and laity, the "city of God" and the "earthly city," requires dismissal of the Church as nothing other than misogynist. Yet in so doing we, like the demons, betray our confusion and the disparagement of our creaturely status and position. We dream to be like God. We would prefer to choose our own path and vocations, determine our own place in divine order, elect our own authorities, and choose our own saviour. All this is the error of demons.

No matter what the venue, false doctrine compromises all the lovely attributes of God. A right and true view of Him is to humankind's benefit and not His own. Belief shaped by an obscured view of our Maker amounts to the worship of a different god. The Father's Word reveals truths about His divine and sacred identity informing us about the stunning extent of His wondrous countenance towards humankind. His attributes explain and impress upon us the limitless extents of His unmatchable grace. Teaching

---

11. In other words, one cannot deduce from the Priesthood of all believers, that all believers are priests. On the question of women's ordination a worldly logic of a single-lensed hermeneutic and single-planed worldview asserts that, if distinctions of sex make no difference outside of the Church (e.g. in society as an incident of the kingdom of the Left) then they should neither make any difference inside. But the historic and apostolic Church has not ordained men *because* they are men. Instead, ordained men represent, re-represent and even *manifest* the presence of the Bridegroom before His Bride; a husband before his wife in heterosexual union. The mutual relationship is characterized by the ideals of servanthood and obedience, which, though they find a correspondence in masculinity and femininity, surpass all the sinful dynamics of power politics caused by the fall from Eden.

falsities regarding His perfect holiness and divine mercy is detrimental to us creatures—and not the Creator.

+ + +

The times may change, but the Word remains constant and immutable. Yet some of these aforesaid issues are not nearly as new as they may at first seem. The Church fought against the Gnostic Gentiles, who are—for those of us who are not ethnically Jewish—our forefathers. They too were moral relativists: 'my' morality was not necessarily 'yours' and 'everything was okay.' There were gods and goddesses, priests and priestesses—an unequivocal celebration of religious diversity. Homosexuality was an accepted practice, and children were sexual acquisitions of the rich and educated. Gnosticism taught that the body was both of no value (and religion was reduced to the pursuit of pure philosophical thought and stoicism) and that the body was of the utmost importance and could one day be immortalized. The results were either hedonism or asceticism. Both confounded the Biblical distinction and relation between body and soul. Let us not flatter ourselves with the claim that we are "progressive" in sexual morality. The difference is that, for the last several hundred years, the Church stood opposed with one unified voice—until recently. With few exceptions, the ecumenical movement lacks interest in touching upon these sorts of integral moral questions. In any case, it seems that the only sexual perversion which both the Western world and the entire Church agree is sin is necrophilia—but for how long?

> The ancient Dragon is their foe;
> His envy and his wrath they know.
> It always is his aim and pride
> Thy Christian people to divide.
> As he of old deceived the world
> And into sin and death has hurled,
> So he now subtly lies in wait
> To ruin school and Church and State.
>
> A Roaring lion, round he goes,
> No halt nor rest he ever knows;
> He seeks the Christians to devour
> And slay them in his dreadful power.
>
> But watchful is the angel band

The World According to *der Zeitgeist*

That follows Christ on every hand
To guard His people where they go
And break the counsel of the Foe.[12]

---

12. TLH 254.

The Purpose Driven Lie

And he said to them, "I saw Satan fall like lightning from heaven." (Luke 10:18)

Remember the former Jehovah Witness who was repulsed by Christian art? Ironically, she herself was a talented artist. But much like the Flemish painters who were influenced by iconoclastic abolitions of religious imagery, she had limited herself to naturalistic landscapes, flowers and other still lifes. After being convinced by the logic of the second council of Nicea of 787 AD, along with some help from the Holy Spirit, this novice painter began to draw fascinating and engaging scenes of Christ affixed to the cross. The most moving portrayal displayed a young melancholy girl embraced by a consoling Jesus as they exchanged loving glances at the foot of His cross. Sadly, months later, catalyzed by a moment of demonic oppression that resulted in a terrible fit of violent rage, she impetuously ripped her canvas to shreds, to her sincere regret once the paroxysm had passed. Yet the fact that she felt free to create a painting of a compassionate and good God holding her in His gentle arms marked a breakthrough in her spiritual maturity and healing.

Many of these individuals whom I had been called to shepherd were shackled by deficiencies to their mental faculties. Whether or not these ailments were the cause or the symptoms of what sometimes appeared to be demonic oppression is near impossible to determine. One woman to whom I provided care escaped from a mental institution and called me from a payphone, begging me to assure her that she was not eternally damned, which is what the voices in her head were telling her. Sometimes I wonder whether or not mental illness and demonic possession/oppression are simultaneously present in a patient.[1] The indeterminable does not dampen the need for a common remedy. Real demons or just delusions of the mind can be equally injurious. Counselling was once conducted exclusively by those of the cloth. Today their skills are often abhorred. Although "holistic therapy" tarries as the mental-health mantra uttered by all reputable helping professionals, the aforesaid issues have all but been transferred entirely from the realm of spirituality to chemistry. In a world in which the two realms of eternal and temporal realities have been forcibly collapsed into one, it remains unsurprising that counselling is conducted almost exclusively by psychiatrists, psychologists and social workers, while their clients are usually advised not to seek services from "biased" Christian faith practitioners. This all happens in spite of the fact that seventy-percent of clients seeking counselling struggle with issues of guilt, forgiveness and God.[2]

There are, however, instances of the medical and religious communities working together in triage. Because an accurate diagnosis in cases of demonic possession is one of the greatest challenges for exorcists, the late Father Candido Amantini, one of the chief exorcists for the Vatican, worked side-by-side with psychiatrists and doctors, and in close consultation with their medical records.[3] He also preferred to use the word "blessing" instead of "exorcism" and "negativity" instead of "possession" in an effort to address the accompanying stigma for "patients" undergoing "treatment."[4] Besides that, he followed the ancient rites.

For the most part, a visit to the priest is normally the troubled soul's last resort since medical doctors are the demigods of modern societies. In spite of the historical revisionism of institutions like the BBC, religious ministers have an outstanding reputation for attending to both the spiritual and physical health of individuals. Sensationalizing the ignominies of the exceptions appeases viewers. The most honourable aspects of the state welfare system were engineered by the Church. Still, the word "pastor" has almost become a euphemism for all that an educated society deplores. Incidentally, the techniques of, and justification for, the religious inquisitions, which were never intended as punitive but were aimed at saving the soul by butchering the body, are uncannily similar to the rehabilitation methods used in insane asylums today. Even fire and heat through electric shock

1. Koch 97.
2. Walsh, *Strengthening Family Resilience*, 49.
3. Amorth, *An Exorcist*, 92.
4. Amorth, *More Stories*, 150.

treatment have enjoyed a recent comeback. Mental health workers may be well-meaning, but many do not hold the same presuppositions regarding the sanctity of life as do the clergy. The Christian tactic used by faithful priests was framed and summarized in the following way: "Confess your sins, repent and receive forgiveness." *That* amounted to therapy. And it was effective. It brought peace to millions of ill souls and healing balm to damaged minds. Today the following words presuppose each clinical session: "You have no sins, you are a good person, do whatever you feel is right as long as you take ownership for it." The business of counselling and life-coaching never lack a retinue of repeat customers. The line between positive thinking and wishful thinking is a fine one. Yet a good attitude will only get one so far.

As a young University student I found myself surreptitiously in my first confession box without even realizing it. Growing up Lutheran amongst heavily pietistic churches unwittingly influenced by the views of Philip Spener and his peers, local ministers seemed terrified at the thought of anyone actually taking them up on their offer expounded in the chapter entitled *Individual Confession and Absolution* in the catechism. I was a faithful recipient of the practice of *public* absolution since it occurred during each Divine Service. But I had never fully comprehended the inexhaustible value of *private* confession. However irrational, I was burdened with sins that I had indeed confessed many a time and knew off by heart. I still felt bad. Notwithstanding an intellectual awareness that all of my loathsome iniquities had already been forgiven, my thoughts remained preoccupied: how could my regrets still haunt me with their nocuous guilt?

One day, arriving early for class, I haphazardly met a priest who was the college chaplain in a corridor of the building. After engaging in cordial conversation, he kindly invited me into his office, which provided a more tasteful setting for our verbal exchange. After a lengthy one-sided conversation, his empathetic listening—neither accusing nor excusing—was followed by a few simple words on God's forgiveness and grace. All of a sudden, something had changed. I felt—well—*light*! Loads of weight had been lifted off my back. It was only many days later that I realized what had happened on that random weekday: I had undergone a private confession—and without any cognizance on my part! If it wasn't for the deplorable higher criticism taught by a liberal priest at the same college and my professor who questioned the necessity for belief in the physical resurrection of

Christ during my *Introduction to the Synoptic Gospels* course, I might have converted to Roman Catholicism.

Many people confuse self-examination with a sadomasochistic introspection. Certainly, exposing one's heart to the mirror of the Decalogue is essential. But many Christians stop there. According to St. Paul in his second letter to the Corinthians, self-examination is a testing to determine whether or not we are "in the faith" (2 Cor 13:5). It is a confession of creedal faith and reliance on Jesus, and not an appeal to innocence or a restatement of guilt. If you dig for dirt in a muddy ground, you are sure to find plenty.

One reason why exorcists must demonstrate exceptional humility and undergo the cleansing of individual confession in preparation for the performance of their duties is that the fear of secrets revealed can easily be used by demons as a weapon against them. The enemy knows many of our hidden sins and will maliciously unveil them by the mouth of the demoniac to both the exorcist's embarrassment and shame.[5] What is remarkable is that he can only repeat *unrepented* sins that remain *unconfessed*. In the case of a priest who was a sceptic observer during an exorcism, a demon decided to verbally promulgate intimate details of his secret love affair to everyone in the room. After humiliating the priest the exorcist commanded the demon to provide an explanation for this harassment technique. The demon was heard stating, "Sins already confessed I do not know."[6] In other words, when sins are forgiven it is as if they had never happened. While the Gospel obliterates sins, the devil is a skilled herald of the Law. By polishing this mirror and lodging it before our consciences, Satan prods us to wallow in the muck of guilt, shame, filth and sin, even under a pious and holy guise that we may mistake for authentic "confession." The adversary can no longer accuse us in the court of God, so he descends into the hidden battlefield of our minds by attempting to condemn those who are already justified with their failures or to excuse them with their successes.

The devil is a slanderer of the faithful. He convinces believers that they are bad parents, bad children, bad spouses, bad workers, bad pastors, with the single goal of decimating our faith and destroying our salvation. The conscience is a delicate instrument. Most people confuse their conscience with their personal preferences and temperamental moods. But having a "good conscience" involves the estimation of others and God. "Baptism, which corresponds to this, now saves you, not as a removal of dirt from

---

5. Vogl 31.
6. Ibid.

the body but as an appeal to God for a good conscience, through the resurrection of Jesus Christ" (1 Peter 3:21). The Judge declares me righteous through the blood of the Lamb shed for my washing and drinking. No room remains for demonic accusations or doubt. My conscience *is* clear as Jesus advocates at my side. My prayers *are* fragrant aromas as Jesus offers them from His altar. I *am* a good and faithful servant as I ride on Jesus the servant-king. The presence of God is a consuming fire, which incinerates the uncleanliness of my identity. My self collides with His, as I am immersed into a theophany of His hidden glory in His Gospel word and sacraments. Faith believes what is present, though unseen. Even the third use of the Law loses its sting for those made righteous, since sanctification describes what the justifying spirit is *already* doing in a life in Christ. In short, "If God is for us, who can be against us?" (Rom 8:31b). Confessing my sins or the abuses of others against me is always prayed in the anticipation of hearing an indubitable affirmation and not a word of condemnation. Absolution is pure joy because it affirms the wonderful unchanging truth.

Spiritual counselling and holy absolution are two planes of the same door, hung together on Christ their hinge. Because of the Office of the Ministry, the pastor boldly promises, "My forgiveness is Christ's. I, therefore, forgive you all your sins in the name of the Father, and of the Son + and of the Holy Spirit." If this were not among the most astounding expressions of Jesus' incarnational presence today, it would be the most preposterous, arrogant and devilish declaration imaginable. How can a mere creature claim to forgive offenses against almighty God? It is blasphemy—a claim to divinity (Mark 2:7)! And yet Jesus remains in the flesh. As a called and ordained servant of the Word, the words that I speak are God's very own words, for He has given them to me to tell. Naturally, the demons flee in terror.

Once upon a time a genuflection occurred at the enrapturing and world-altering words of the Nicene Creed, "He was made man." Upon hearing them, devils squirm as their ears burn. God suffered for us in history under Pontius Pilate. He was crucified, died and was buried. Even non-Christian historians and contemporaries of the apostles like Titus Flavius Josephus, though refusing to believe in the resurrection, were mystified by the empty tomb. Unlike some religions that lack a historical foundation supported by credible scholarly research and archaeological discovery, the fact that the man Jesus of Nazareth was crucified and buried is historical fact. Doubts are unfounded. The demons are well aware of this historical reality, and shudder (Jas 2:19). "He was made man." Divine invigorating power flows from the Office of the Ministry as God remains man and with man. The miraculous power and gift common to all faithful pastors is even more phenomenal than the ability to raise the dead: the ability to forgive sins (John 20:22-23)! At His ascension, Jesus only disappeared from human sight. His flesh is still offered in His Holy Communion. Yet it remains invisible, hidden under bread and wine. It is also concealed in people. His ministers are His oracles. He remains unseen but still heard. We may take the words delivered from the pulpit for granted, but hell shivers at their utterance.[7]

Ironically, the trajectory of our culture's glorification of the individual has derided the practice of private confession. I suppose that *public* confession is considered to be safer. We prefer anonymity. One can stealthily hide one's secret sins from the listening man. But although the two offer the same thing, they are not identical. Besides the spiritual benefits obtained through a personal encounter with the holy wounds of our vicarious Redeemer, the practice itself is pedantic, ameliorating an often belated honest self-awareness. Our vanity frequently deters us from a comprehensive and detailed confession. At the very least, we hesitate. The sinful human disposition is to assume that others think and behave just as we do. Children are gullible because they are more innocent than we are. We lack trust in others, because we are untrustworthy ourselves. We assume that they will gossip, because we ourselves find the temptation irresistible. Remembering the naked patriarch Noah in his drunken stupor after the flood, clothed by two sons but mocked by one, we agonize over what sort of reception we will receive at the hand of our judge. Those who scorn private confession discard the concept of a confidant because they fear that he will somehow judge them differently in his other dealings with them; that the priest will remember their insidious sins and even verbally repeat them regardless of divine promises made to the contrary. After all, knowledge is power.

In the eighteenth-century, Friedrich D. E. Schleiermacher, hailed as the father of modern theology, had convinced the Christian world that ecclesiastical dogmas and ecumenical councils were untrustworthy sources for Biblical hermeneutics. Instead, the individual was the only truly reliable interpreter. Yet, if faith is trust, and trust believes what someone else tells you, then what is the spiritual impact of this supercilious reluctance to trust

---

7. Conversely, when the pastor's words are inconsistent with the Holy Scriptures and fail to properly distinguish between the Law and the Gospel, they become the devil's instrument. The ministers that speak them are, no matter how undeliberate, "antichrists."

our Lord's stewards with God's mandate to keep us saved? Jesus promises, "The one who hears you hears me, and the one who rejects you rejects me, and the one who rejects me rejects him who sent me" (Luke 10:16). Confessing sins to strangers, who we assume must consider themselves morally and spiritually superior to ourselves, actuates accusations of outdated and fanatical religion. Yet as the demon in C.S. Lewis' *The Screwtape Letters* pensively observes: "A moderate religion is as good for us as no religion at all—and more amusing."[8] Incidentally, even uncle Screwtape and his nephew Wormwood didn't chat on a first name basis.

It is a perplexing trend of our convoluted age that formalities have been lost, and titles are often no longer applied. Uniforms mean little today. Those who insist on being addressed as "doctor" or "pastor" followed by a surname, and not a given name, are viewed as conceited. Children speak to their elders as if they are their equals. Many clergy robe up in albs and chasubles for aesthetic reasons alone. Ties are chosen over clerical collars, unless fashion dictates otherwise. Nonetheless, ecclesiastical titles point to something other than the one who holds them. Cassocks, stoles and other priestly attire are costumes that hide the individual and proclaim the Office of Christ. When one is physically unwell, one finds a greater measure of comfort in knowing that one's surgeon has been adequately trained, than one does in knowing that he or she prefers to be addressed on a first name basis. Our souls are sick. Pastors do more than represent Christ, they *re-present* Christ. They speak for Him. They stand in His stead: "And by the command of my Lord Jesus Christ, I forgive you all your sins. . ." Otherwise, the Office of the holy Ministry has been hijacked by a gang of imposters. Rightfully, written homilies are carefully scrutinized before their delivery to the Lord's people. Besides, it is not the residing minister's letter. Sermons are printed, read or memorized, because errors can kill. Homilies are the words of the Groom to His Bride. The priest ensues as messenger and ambassador. The playful sharing of personal anecdotes during worship by an overly friendly pastor, who loathes formalities by insisting that they raise barriers to developing healthy personal relationships, only distracts his hearers from Christ the Lord. Pastors hide themselves behind liturgical furniture such as fonts, lecterns and altars, so that the focus on them is lessened, and, instead, worshippers are more inclined to hear the Word of God.

The mentally oppressed are not the only ones bombarded by multiple voices. Satan tempts us all to listen to the voices of reason, the heart, feelings

---

8. Lewis, *The Screwtape Letters*, 28.

The Purpose Driven Lie

and a myriad of disparate Biblical interpretations. Yet there is only one voice that provides certainty within this ubiquity of suffering: the Word of God spoken from the lips of mother Church. Accordingly, the servants of the Church are identical in appearance: they resonate *the same* "sound," reciting from *the same* lectionary, repeating the *same message*, because they are re-presenters of a God who is One, "the same yesterday, and today and forever" (Heb 13:8). His message never changes and is applicable to all people of all times and places. Because God does not suffer from multi-personality disorder, innovations to His means of salvation are always dangerous for us. Pastors who are irreverent and careless in handling the holy things of God have forgotten that they are servants in another man's living room and cooks in another chef's kitchen. They are spiritually treacherous. Although our society is roused and enticed by the cult of personality, every religious incident of such is idolatry. Few worshippers attribute great sermons to a beloved minister's seminary education or to the dogmas of his Church. Inadvertently, he himself gets the credit. The promise that a pastor does not minister in his own stead is a pacifying comfort to him as well. Otherwise accusatory feelings of personal accountability when church membership declines, faithful attendees turn mutinous and new ones quit dissatisfied, pose a tiring unrelenting challenge. A pastor's temptations towards self-debasement and self-promotion find a common origin in the same diabolical confusion between his personal identity and his priestly one.

The Lord considers the holy ministry the highest of callings because those who fill the Office are stewards of the mysteries of His Son (1 Cor 4:1), administrators and bureaucrats of His holy kingdom. Indeed every vocation is holy. But through this one believers are equipped for their own holy ministry and priesthood, which penetrate their respective vocations. The Divine Call is not a reward for the most pious. The people who are pastors are powerless. They merely work in the cubicles of the celestial company, a mighty corporation indeed. The devil may not fear the employees but he fears the CEO. Because of Jesus' Office, we clergy "beat down Satan under our feet,"[9] as prayed in the Litany. "As it is written, 'How beautiful are the feet of those who preach the good news!'" (Rom 10:15). The seraphim touch our lips with the burning coal from a blood-stained altar (Isa 6:6–8) and, from the pulpit, set the world ablaze with His invincible Word of love.

Thus, because of their Office, pastors are powerful even when they are unappreciated or despised. "The kingdom of God has come near you" (Luke

---

9. LSB 289.

10:9) for better or for worse: "To one a fragrance from death to death, to the other a fragrance from life to life" (2 Cor 2:16)! Although these humble servants are mere clerks they are also shareholders and co-workers with the Lord (1 Cor 3:9). Moreover, these prayerful administrators of God's grace are His children and heirs (Rom 8:17). The devil may forcefully enlist others to do his work as slaves, but God invites us to work with Him as friends. Nothing can hinder the success of this family-run business. The imperious anti-clericalism that pretentiously seeks to terminate an undistinguished pastor's "contract" does no good. The hiring of an admired "gifted" preacher because of his eloquent elocution changes nothing.[10] Expanding the massive myriad of often unusual and contradictory expectations laid upon a humble shepherd is futile. Faithful pastors may be penalized for favouring rigid manuscripts over extemporaneous preaching yet woe to those who reject their shepherds and transform their ministry into a toilsome labour (Luke 10:10–12).

The close connection between the Lord and His representatives is delineated by Christ's promise and warning: "He who hears you hears me" (Luke 10:16). The Corinthians thought that St. Paul was difficult to get along with. Moreover, his preaching put Eutychus to sleep causing a fatal fall from a three-storey window. The disciples were no heroes. The efficacy of the Office is never fixed in the individual. We know little about the lives of the apostles. Consider St. Matthias who replaced Judas by lot: unnoticed and forgotten, likely because he quietly and meekly performed his pastoral duties. He was only doing what He was asked to do, seeking no glory for himself or heavenly rewards. Of what personal accomplishment can any man boast (Gal 6:14)? God is good. Those who hold the Office are not. They only distribute good things.

Pastors who cave in to the temptation to personalize their ministry by highlighting the effectiveness of their unique aptitudes in advancing the Gospel have foolishly forsaken their agency as deliverers of divine parcels. Linguist, Noam Chomsky, argues that language is the unique expression of a human creature's identity. The song of our soul resonates through the melody of our speech. A disharmonious Christian spirit discloses its

---

10. It is frightening how easily many people will believe anything said with enough confidence and conviction regardless of its veracity. However, although the packaging may be an effective mechanism for selling a product, it does not necessarily accurately and truthfully represent its content. For instance, most people judge sermons based upon their delivery (i.e. the "packaging" of effective public speaking) and not their content (i.e. how well they proclaim the Gospel of Christ and Him crucified).

disorientation with the tune of God's Holy Spirit in every ungainly word. Applied to clergy, if we talk the way we think, then cool and casual pastors, who are so comfortable in the pulpit that they no longer even use one, betray an insolent mindset that is indifferent towards Him with whom they share a holy ground. Nevertheless, God blesses their ministry in spite of themselves, for again, the validity of the pastoral office is not contingent upon the holiness of its bishops.

Accordingly, the sacraments remain efficacious even in the scandalous case of an evil and faithless individual usurping the holy Office. The means of grace bring Christians to a portal that leads to a heavenly bliss untold. Sadly, most of those with whom I have practiced confession and offered absolution are mentally ill, demonically oppressed, or incarcerated in prison. Unlike the rest of us, these are the ones who have a most difficult time hiding their sins. Yet Jesus calls them the most blessed of all (Matt 5:3).

+ + +

One literary theme of Russian author Fyodor Dostoevsky's novels is that crazy people are the sanest. They should be admired for their honest assessment of themselves and their frankness in confessing their needs. French thinker Michel Foucault argues that they are secretly envied since they are permitted to get away with what the rest of proper folk are not allowed.[11] In antiquity the mentally ill were an accepted and tolerated subgroup of society, existential reminders of the overall incompleteness of our irresolute world. Today we hide them away, repulsed. We justify these prisons as incubators for *their* safety. In reality, we build these institutions to calm *our* nerves and soothe *our* fears. Deep down, we want all forms of poverty concealed. Ignorance is bliss. Hurting people are downers. Lines of credit are only one of the many creative institutionalized methods of fabricating the fantastic illusion that we are happy, stable, self-sufficient and rich. Convalescent homes help too. Cosmetics offer us a false, but welcome, sense of normalcy since none of us look exceptionally attractive in the morning. Third-world societies cannot afford to live as dishonestly. A low life-expectancy rate does not discriminate between poor and rich. Other peoples' problems are everyone's business. In Haiti, for instance, public

---

11. Foucault, *Madness and Civilization*, 23.

displays of demon possession are not uncommon.[12] Unlike us, they lack sufficient funds to lock away their demoniacs.

Voodoo culture represents one benighted attempt to gain control and enhance one's status in this poorest country of the Western hemisphere. Whether or not the witchdoctors have ever eaten their babies while under a trance does not change the intensity of the danger. The cost of accumulating power is always high. Fear of the future, economic frustration and psychological depression are fuel for a devil that is not shy in flaunting his services. Most Haitians believe in God and the devil. They are just not sure whether the former is the more useful of the two. Manichaeism—the belief in two warring deities, one good and one evil—poses no temptation. Doubting God's loving promise does (Rom 8:31). Haitians know that God is omnipotent but many are unsure whether or not He really cares about them. In our "advanced" wealthy society, which caricatures demons as comical mythological cartoons, the evil gang has adopted a different strategy. They prefer to remain undercover. The disbelief in their existence by the educated and self-righteous is in the tyrant's best interest. Again, only crazy people believe in the devil, right?

Is not the hyper-individualism of today's society at least partially the cause for our puritanical and merciless flight from exposure to sickness, death and the neurosis of others? Canadian political philosopher, Charles Taylor, coined the term "atomistic" for our inability to behave in communitarian ways.[13] Such libertarianism is encountered both in and outside the Church. Sinners are self-serving. For some the Church has become a

---

12. Displays of the supernatural are common throughout the developing world where the seeds of the Gospel have been sown for the first time and a deepening faith in the God who performs the miracles is the most likely result. Missionaries often hesitate in sharing stories in the "developed" nations due to the prevalence of rationalism, even among Christian clergy who often mistake the supernatural with superstition. While I was visiting a church in India, a pastor told how a group of visiting ministers from America thought how "cute" it would be to receive a blessing from a Hindu priest during a visit to a temple. They all fell ill afterwards. During the same trip, Christian witnesses shared with me a case where the arm of an amputee was miraculously restored in church. They could even feel it flinging past them through an open window during worship. Such stories boggle the scientific mind, but our doubts often expose our underpinning belief system, and our hidden gods. One church in Indonesia had no access to wine for the Holy Sacrament and so water was habitually transformed by God as was the case at Cana. Koch 114. These represent only a tiny known sample of miracles today. Yet our Lord continues to remind us all: "Blessed are those who have not seen and yet have believed" (John 20:29).

13. Taylor, *Sources of the Self*, 82.

communion with God with little direct involvement with others. Coffee fellowship doesn't count. For others church is a means of social networking and a lot cheaper than the on-line dating services. In short, an assembly of individuals congregated together is not necessarily identical to a community.

Society today exhibits a relationship of convenience rather than expressing a shared *ethos*. Accordingly, "What do I have to do with a prisoner, a stranger, the mentally insane?" We would rather lock the undesirables away. We gain nothing from them. They embarrass us. Even worse, they are reminders of the profusion of disagreeable possibilities within our own life destinations. *We* could become like *them*. In the case of the mentally ill, they put a damper on our optimism by reminding us that, to some degree, irrationality is unpreventable. We wish that they were never born. Partial-birth abortion is infanticide, even when we label it an after-birth medical procedure. Yet there is still hope. Post-modern thinkers, such as Jacques Derrida, argue that although some specialized language is necessary for efficient functioning in modern society, a lot of it unnecessarily excludes the lay populace from the dialogue. The specialists possess the means of production. But they never totally succeed. Consumers were still appalled by allegations of the use of aborted fetal tissue in Pepsi, Kraft and Nestle products. Oddly, vaccines were less controversial. And, still, secular society objects that religious people are the nonsensical ones.

But what is the definitive line between irrationality and insanity? For us "normal" people, who believe ourselves to be immune from irrational thought, our craziness is harder to detect. However, incidents of insanity have the potential as acting as our own watchdogs, if we allow them. We insisted that we would never again entertain the science of eugenics, perpetuated by most of the industrialized nations prior to WWII, even though it epitomized a natural logical conclusion to the Darwinian dictum of survival of the fittest. This underlying philosophical principle partially drove the Nazi agenda to exterminate all those deemed undesirable. Incidentally, ninety-percent of children diagnosed with Down's syndrome are aborted. We hide away our undesirables or destroy them. This is crazy. We change the names of medical conditions and controversial procedures in order to avoid stigma and fool our opponents. This is unreasonable. Only a few are privy to the hidden agenda. Demons like secrets too. They dwell in dark places. Foucault's deconstructionism draws parallels between mental institutions and prisons: the use of medication, punishment, uniforms, to name a few. C.S Lewis argues that treating crime as an illness is a dehumanizing insult to the felon.[14] The murderer makes an educated decision. Why conjecture that he was driven by madness? Does evidence of a neglected childhood alleviate his guilt? In its denial of sin, the world prefers to label villains as delinquents. Behaviourism has renamed prisons as "correctional services." Prison sentences are corrective, even didactic, and no longer punitive. Public displays of punishment were effective means of dissuasion because they awakened a sense of shame in criminals who felt themselves personally responsible. Today no one is guilty, they are all just sick. Convicts are "cases" that require a little more moral fine-tuning than the rest of us. Reform is the answer as punishment was the cause. Preventative behaviour management has replaced restorative justice, illustrating the subtle shift of power from unseen forces that we cannot control, such as the existence of evil and sin, to ones that we can: education and medicine. Since reason is a gift of God intended for the just and orderly operation of society, it comes of no surprise that even here the devil exerts his influence of confusing logic, knowledge and power.

+ + +

I once made a pastoral visit to a mental hospital where a teenage member of our parish dolefully found a permanent lodging. As per usual, I wore my clerical collar. A spirit of unequivocal immaturity and disrespect betrayed the staff's prejudice towards this unaccustomed visit from a priest. "I guess you're here to do an exorcism—there's the line-up," chuckled one nurse with a malicious grin as she pointed to some languid patients sitting lethargically in a room behind bars and thick glass. After all, why on earth would a religious minister visit the mentally insane unless to perform an exorcism? For the unchurched, Hollywood movies remain their main source of information. Aloof, the nurse continued to brand her patients as "irrational," "hopeless" and "lost causes." Granted, they do lack some of their reasoning capacities. So the critics said of Jesus, "He has a demon, and is insane; why listen to him?" (John 10:20) Meanwhile, some of the staff could have benefited from a pastoral visit themselves. I am sure that their chaplain had stories too. But what struck me most about the hospital personnel was their deep-rooted cynicism. Perhaps their jaded sarcasm and tasteless humour were a coping mechanism after years of working in that

---

14. Lewis, "The Humanitarian Theory of Punishment," 97.

depressing environment. Hence, once again, some of the staff could have benefited from a pastoral visit themselves. In any case, these marginalized patients were some of the "least of these" with whom Jesus spent a lot of His time. I, for one—head hung in shame—had not. Thank God that the measure of heavenly grace displayed towards us does not rest upon the quality of our good deeds, since we never have much to show.

One redeemable quality of the institutionalized insane is their flexible schedule. No one and nothing competes with their time. Some are desperate to hear the sweet Gospel that God has not forgotten them and that a better world awaits them. Others are bored and eager to listen to just about anyone. They make an easy church. When God asks someone to His house for supper, one would think that that invitation would take priority over every other. Yet in our twisted world, the parable of the wedding banquet—when the invitees not only decline the invitation but also kill the king's servants (Matt 22:1–14)—best typifies the most common response. In any case, these inmates have no other invitations with which to contend. Scheduling quandaries with hockey or soccer practice, Sunday work commitments, eager insistence on maintaining shut-in status—all of which remain tiring and unconvincing excuses for withering church attendance—were never at play in my ventures to the hospital. The staff may be sceptics but the mentally disturbed are receptive. Most are entirely mindful that they have dire needs, while many sane people deny theirs. Some were tragically immersed in the occult as a plausible cause of their admittance, while the rest of us, though "free," still have our own demons to contend with.

The bottom line is: none of them belong. Like the rest of us, all of them seek peace. Demonic activity is characterized by a lack of peace. The demon-possessed are flustered and edgy. Exorcism touches on "sacred space" by its mere proximity to the spiritual realm. Despite the implicit claims of *Chicken Soup for the Soul*, not all spirituality is godly. Demons remain angels, albeit corrupted and perverted. But they have chosen no longer to behave like angels, serve like angels, nor worship like angels. Their anti-churches are often filled with people, but are temples in which the Holy Spirit never, or no longer, resides. A faithful pastor entering that temple in order to cleanse it of these intruders, arrives into an arena with which he may be very unfamiliar and rightly uncomfortable. Despite the absence of constitutions, registries and offering plates, churches are planted in mental institutions, hospitals and prisons whenever prayers are recited and sacramental rites occur. Jesus' incarnational presence creates the church. The means of grace manifest it. Displays of angered outbursts, bitter cries and violent eruptions pose no hindrance to the work of the one living God. In regular churches, Christians have devised polite ways of screaming at their pastors too. Yet through the Church the song goes on.

+ + +

The true Church in no way resembles its demonic imitations. The tempo of Divine Service is reverently slow, orderly and calm, and rightfully so. Christ prayed quietly. He *silenced* demons. Elijah heard God in a whisper. Silence is undervalued because our culture is prone to noise. Worship does not necessitate solitude, but, still, it ought to create a serene environment and allow for tranquil reflection, which is often cultivated by prolonged periods of silence. In politics, what is not said is as important as that which is said. The same holds true in holy conversation. Liturgists who move too quickly while performing their sacred duties, neglect to whisper while the faithful pray, or inadvertently rupture a reverential pulse attuned to that of the heavenly pace, precipitate a tone that too closely resembles the rhythm of our regular life. Instead, "Be still and know that I am God" (Ps 46:10). It sounds easy. We make it hard, since doing nothing (i.e. being silent and still) is recurrently equated with laziness. Needless to say, the enemy would have us believe that nothing in life is free.

For the sake of the laity in church (who are God's guests after all) I continue to have reservations about the use of lay readers in worship. It is hard to "be still" when tasked to do something. I have often wondered whether or not the suggestion that God needs help in Divine Service might also lead to a doubt in the monergism of grace: that our Lord is able to save us all by Himself. Besides, reading in public is more demanding than it may first appear. Doing it well requires training and deliberation. The devil detests the public proclamation of Scripture. Accordingly, God's conduits are routinely attacked and distracted. Presiding over the liturgy is strangely exhausting, even when it is of short duration. Liturgical worship cannot be reduced to a sequence of distinctive acts delegated to enthusiastic volunteers. It is an uninterrupted materialization of one single spiritual battle in an all-encompassing spiritual war. The weaponry is a "deposit" that has stood the test of time (2 Tim 1:14). Pastors are soldiers. Lay people fight faithfully as well, but this is not their bunker to defend.

The Purpose Driven Lie

Rumour has it that mandating lay readers is a way of helping people feel like they are participating in the church service. Those who perpetrate the argument are governed by a misguided objective for the Divine Service. Namely, besides responding in thanksgiving during the liturgy, lay people are not supposed to "participate" outside of simply receiving Christ's holy gifts. They are tired, beaten and bruised after a week of spiritual war. They have come to church not to serve, but *to be* served in an oasis prepared for them in the midst of their battlefields. Mary chose the good part and sat still and quiet at the feet of Jesus as *He* spoke to *her* (Luke 10:38–42). Martha was busy looking for ways to serve Him. There was a time to work, but this was not it. A sick patient is not expected to administer his or her own intravenous. The pastor serves and the congregation receives. To do nothing during mass may feel awkward—as awkward as Christ washing the disciples' feet on Maundy Thursday—but it is, nonetheless, normal and spiritually healthy. Moreover, it is good news. It shows God's persistent commitment to washing our feet while we sit back and relax. Sabbath means "rest." The commandment to observe the Sabbath is certainly unique. It asks man to do nothing. The author of the letter to the Hebrews considers all days as holy since Christians reside in a state of grace in the final chapter of history. To emphasize the pivotal point, the Church moved the holy day from Saturday to Sunday, not only in appreciation of the New Testament era that the resurrection had ushered in (i.e. the unleashing of a new life visualized by the beginning of a new week), but also to send a message to the Jews and Sabbatarians who wanted to make the Sabbath rest about *doing* something (such as the work of *observing* a day for worship).

Yet even in light of all of this, the devil still manages to transform worship into a burden, as God's children, who desperately require His service, begrudgingly make their way to His house. Unmindful that they are in fact God's honoured guests invited to recline at table with Him, many labour with the tiring insistence that church ought to include more of their own participation: "After all, isn't religion about giving?" To the contrary, Christ says that it is about receiving. There is one moment in the workweek that we are asked to do nothing but sit, rest and listen, and we restless creatures still manage to seek ways to turn a *divine service* for man into a *human service* for God. In fairness, it is not that to which we are accustomed. But the food isn't the problem; rather, it is our own appetite. So, contemporary music in church satisfies our itching ears as it approximates worship with that which we are already comfortable. The temptation is to apply the same logic to the message. To recapitulate, it is not our service with which to tamper. We are guests in another man's home. Video clips in lieu of sermons probably take greater liberties than those which our Lord allows in His stead. Jesus said that He came not to be served, but to serve (Matt 20:28). The old King James Version uses the word "minister" instead of "serve" intricately connecting the pastoral office with His own. God serves His cherished guests in Divine Service through His called servants. Do we believe Him? If so, resistance towards a perception of the lay role as something other than an intimately serene reclining at a banquet fit for angels ought to dwindle. What is it about the singularity of the pastoral office that offends? When church tires us we may as well relax at home. Confused and sometimes angry Christians protest, "We can serve God anywhere!" Curiously, God does not behave as we do. But demons do.

+ + +

It is uncanny how similar the fallen angels are to us. They even attend church oftentimes. Demonic activity is not alien to some "Christian" worship despite the sincerity of worshippers. Even signs, wonders, miracles and other instances of success and victory over Satan's kingdom are no guarantee of the presence of God: "On that day many will say to me, 'Lord, Lord, did we not prophesy in your name, and cast out demons in your name, and do many mighty works in your name?" (Matt 7:22). A charismatic preacher of a large and growing Christian community once confessed that he himself had difficulty deciphering between manifestations of the devil and those of the Holy Ghost. It is a chilling and frightening statement. When a "filling with the Holy Spirit" resembles the possession by a demon or "drunkenness in the Spirit" displays the same symptoms as debauchery, whatever it is that makes a space sacred is obviously amiss. When I hear the hymns of J.S. Bach for instance, I find myself in awe of the majesty of God. The demons are incapable of listening for long. They flee from the divine liturgy and timeless chants of the Church. A reverent tune frames the message that it announces, deepening devotion and inspiring prayer. But it is the conveyed Word that chases the evil away. Nonetheless, let us never underestimate the vital significance of the melody. Canadian philosopher of communication theory Marshall McLuhan has taught us that there are no neutral media. The material principle provides shape to the formal principle. Form includes content. Every medium carries a message—*is* a message. Not only does the message that is conveyed matter. *The way in which* it is conveyed matters as well. Televisions make no distinctions between reality and fantasy, equalizing the value of all news.[15] Accordingly, TV cannot be treated as a serious means of communicating important information. It is good for only one thing: entertainment. Thus, the question is not simply whether "Christian commercials" are an *effective* means of conveying the Gospel but whether or not they are an *appropriate* one. No technology is neutral. This should disturb us. Do microphones dilute the quality of the message? If "faith comes from hearing, and hearing through the word of Christ" (Rom 10:17), does it make any difference whether or not the listener receives the message from an audio signal instead of from the mouth of his or her pastor? It may not, but isn't it worth asking the question? Redesigning the space of a church sanctuary so that the faithful only partially face Christ's altar, or rearranging the furniture to accommodate a drum set, always changes the way one worships.

This is not "high church" elitism. The devil wishes nothing more than to turn Christians away from God's work and back to our own. Defending tradition is partially, admittedly, driven by a slippery slope rationale. But this hill has a treacherously steep incline. Alas, the tempter remains close at the side of every believer. But there will be no displays of frenzied demonic activity when the holy Triune God is rightly worshipped in truth and purity—and in the solemn way of the Fathers. Worship is as fun as war. Church is as entertaining as a hospital. I would rather have an old, ugly, mundane surgeon who is competent in his diagnosis and treatment of my illness, than a young, interesting and fun-loving—incompetent one. The virtues of amusement are overstated. Nevertheless, they remain consistently in line with the values of our consumerist society. American media theorist Neil Postman warns of the dangers of insisting that education be fun.[16] Politicians require a sense of humour if they wish to get elected. No one likes a killjoy. Yet the consummation of a marriage by a virgin couple on the night

---

15. For example, a twenty-second news broadcast covering the murder of a man on a subway is followed by a twenty-second feel-good story depicting a puppy dog catching a Frisbee in the park. This is then interrupted by a thirty-second advertisement for a soft drink. Psychologically, each clip carries the same weight, regardless of variances in the moral gravity of their respective content. We may protest, since we suddenly feel thirsty in the grocery store while we have long forgotten about the murder. The difference is that the advertisements deliberately tap into the three memory banks of the human mind. After sixty years, most viewers are aware of the agenda to "program" us to purchase their products, but how many realize that the majority of news anchors are hired actors too?

16. See Postman, *Amusing ourselves to death*.

of their wedding would not be described as fun. It is much more than that. It is better. It is lovely. It is beautiful.

I have always admired the novels of H.G. Wells in their satirical examination of our positivistic society. Thematically, his stories such as *The Invisible Man* or *The Island of Dr. Moreau* divulge how the volatile technological development driven by Darwinian optimism detaches man from nature and self. Technology is not neutral, and when misunderstood and misused, it dehumanizes. I suppose that the even darker morbid works of Stanley Kubrick do something similar through film. But if being Christian means becoming more human, in the sense of regaining the essence of what it is to live in self-recognition as a creature of God restored through the second Adam Jesus Christ, Christians ought to be wary of innovations that may threaten this spiritually restorative process, such as modifications to the traditional mediums used in church.

In David Cronenberg's horror classic, *The Fly*, the scientist's curious quest to become something that he is not (again, characteristic of the demons), empowered by technological equipment that enables him to overstep his creatureliness as a human being, results in an irreversible monstrous transformation and ineluctable self-destruction. Innovations in the liturgy driven by seemingly harmless technological developments are not only dehumanizing, but "de-Christianizing." When pews were introduced into churches, they unintentionally altered the way in which the worshipper worshipped. Religious architecture matters. Churches were originally designed for one single purpose: a rightly uncomfortable yet glorious encounter with the community of the Divine. Today, we build multifunctional sanctuaries that are easily aligned with the familiarities of ordinary life. Even hymnals blurred the line between churches and schools. Instead of attending worship to receive Christ's holy gifts, people went to learn about the Bible as they were taught by ministers who were viewed as elevated lay people. People no longer go to church to eat at the Lord's altar, but to hear a good sermon.[17] The "thriving" churches of today are designed to resemble college campuses.

The way we do things affects the things we do. Disposable communion cups import the grotesque principles of an accelerating fast-food culture into our cherished spirituality, while individual communion cups misshape the ways in which we think about ourselves as a body. Screens

---

17 This is not intended to devalue the importance of relevant sermons; i.e. good preaching makes us hungry for the Sacrament, or, rather, *proclaims* how hungry we actually are (even when we don't feel it).

in sanctuaries warp our ability to hear the sermon and pray, because of the prominent—and often idolatrous—role that they play in our homes in disconnecting us from the real world. Even the well-meaning video-recording of exorcisms on the internet, intended not to sensationalize but rather to rebuff sceptics, somehow degrades sacred space through the mixing of common and sacrosanct metaphors. The Anglican instruction on exorcism forty years ago advises that anyone unknown to the priest should not be present.[18] That was before the invention of VTC and streaming. Once upon a time, picture taking was forbidden during church services, holy ground viewed as trodden upon by the video camera. There are no neutral media. In reflecting on the typologies of the Old Testament, St. Cyril of Jerusalem wrote that life comes by means of wood.[19] When you think about it, every wooden pew is a tiny reminder of the crucifixion. Metallic theatre seats do not convey the same message. Because theological consequences to adopting new technologies into the life of the Church are unavoidable, we Lutherans should never become too eager in seeking reform, even though they are, obviously, necessary on occasion.

Few pastors are exempt from the temptation to "improve" upon divine and apostolic traditions when the sought-after results are lacking. Clergy of all denominations are inclined to lean on other methods beside the Word of God in making the Church grow or satisfying hungry souls, surrendering to people's "felt needs" in spite of their distance from "real needs." Resorting to tactics that dilute both the Law and the Gospel can be likened to hiding medicine in syrup from unsuspecting children as Mary Poppins advises, "a spoon full of sugar helps the medicine go down." Accordingly, we divulge an attitude of worship not based on truth but utility. If marriage does not satisfy all of a spouse's perceived needs and demands a disproportionate percent of service rendered, it is annulled. Divorce between spouses who fail to contribute an equal percentage of financial or emotional assets to the relationship is considered reasonable by most. A meaningful life, after all, is defined in terms of self-fulfilment. If a product doesn't please, it is returned with a refund. Still, true Christianity announces nothing of greater value than the worship of the one true God. It is every person's priority and the intended object of all their time, energy and funds. Whether we experience a lack of personal victories and still die of cancer, God the maker of heaven and earth, Redeemer, and Sanctifier, is still rightly worshipped. Granted,

---

18. *Exorcism* 35.
19. St. Cyril of Jerusalem, *Catechetical Lectures*, 13: 20–21.

God considers the most honourable worship as our receiving of His service. "If I do not wash you, you have no share with me" (John 13:8b). He who is self-sufficient and lacks nothing does not require our sacrifices and offerings. Rather, "The sacrifices of God are a broken spirit" (Ps 51:17).

The devil may tolerate worshipping God on one's own terms, whether at home, on the beach, or in the park. But he holds in contempt those "traditionalists" who still attend church weekly. Reading about a cure for an infectious disease is not identical to undergoing treatment. Satan is not intimidated by head knowledge about God. It is no coincidence that Sunday is the most taxing day to awake early. Reading one's Bible at home can be likened to reading a menu before the meal is served. It is befitting preparation for the feast to come while, at the same time, whetting one's famished appetite. But, it is not the meal itself. The banquet is reserved for Divine Service and by invitation only. Those who have no interest in the Lord's family, who rhythmically live as if they spurn their host by routinely cutting off ties with His home, have already excommunicated themselves from the means of salvation; their habit of hunger extends itself into eternity regrettably finding its final deposit in hell. An exclusive diet of simple Bible reading in the privacy of one's living room ultimately leaves one unsatisfied and hungry. The devil rejoices at such unknowing fasts.

For those who attend church regularly, the endless disgruntled complaints betray a dual allegiance. We are less anti-cultural than we like to believe. The fuel of capitalism is dissatisfaction and stimulation. Christian consumers, like the rest of our society, are subconsciously conditioned to the belief that big is better. We prefer a large congregation, even though a small one allows for more effective and genuine shepherding. Noah's church consisted of only eight. He was not very popular either. Yet God kept them afloat. Not lacking sagacity, former Pope Benedict XVI apparently predicted that the "church will grow, but will grow smaller"—respite for some, puzzling to most. Moreover, the importation of economic theory into the kingdom of God is manifested in discontent over the meal. Like the Israelites who had grown tired of Manna and had all but lost faith, we wish for a greater selection and more variety. Consumerism presumes product diversity. Churchgoers long for guest speakers. Although repetition equips us to earnestly pray the liturgy instead of casually reading it, we beg for diversity in "banal" worship, boring easily. Innovation is the muscle of capitalism. Mom's home cooking has become tiresome. Unified worship in spirit and truth is obstructed by a buffet-style thinking about our worship life.

This same idolatrous view of worship insists upon a congregation of young people in order to legitimize church. The Old Testament believers upheld the elderly as a great blessing inculcating an unmatchable wisdom to the young. The demons would have us deride advancements in age. The aged are not simply to be tolerated, like an out-dated piece of furniture begging for remodelling. Instead they are precious stones carefully casted in the wall of our Lord's castle among which the rest of us hopefully may one day find a place. A lack of maturity insists that young people require their own pastor in order to "be relevant." What sort of children ask that mom, dad and grandma eat at another time because their dinner and conversation are somehow beneath them? Tragic are the dirges of elderly people who lament that there are not enough young people at table. Yet in spite of their self-deprecation God still calls them blessed.

Forgive the rant, but are the needs of the young and the old that different? Are the forgiveness of sins and the cross of Calvary no longer relevant for believers of all times and in all places? Specialized ministries derived from nebulous vision statements tend to divert the focus from the singular mission of the Church. The true message of the cross is never popular, despite the best efforts of "youth pastors" at making it cool. Desperation packages the gospel with slick goatees and hip outfits without which a faithful shepherd's words are devalued. Inasmuch as they struggle with insecurity and an uncertain self-image exposing them as easy targets to manipulation, teenagers are not that shallow. But adolescence does long to be shaped, molded and influenced. Are youth services not the logical conclusion of Sunday school in churches where it is offered as a substitution for Divine Service? It ought to come as no surprise that children who were consistently babysat during church find it boring after they "graduate" from their confirmation classes. Dwindling numbers are the fault of whom? Jesus says, "Let the little children come to me and do not hinder them, for to such belongs the kingdom of heaven" (Matt 19:14) but some parents prefer their own recess, even at the risk of a millstone tied around their necks (Luke 17:2).

Even well-meaning children's messages wedged within the Divine Service can promote such a generational segregation. Are we not all, both young and old, tiny little children held in the arms of our precious Saviour, merciful Father and kind Brother? We seek divisions, but God makes Christians of only one kind. The hordes of hell must delight over all the despairing and faithless extents undergone to "make relevant" the timeless Gospel to Generation X and Y. Are men's retreats, "mom and tots" activities, and young adults' groups really necessary for a "spirit-filled" church? Are we not *one* bride? Is the Gospel not enough? Jesus prays, "that they may all be one, just as you, Father, are in me, and I in you, that they also may be in us, so that the world may believe that you have sent me" (John 17:21).

What God unites, the devil seeks to divide. Because communities reflect the Trinitarian nature of God they are targets of infernal darts. Demons enjoy no family. They are independent, selfish and highly individualistic, embodying the values of our materialist society. The Satanic Bible by Anton Szandor LaVey consists not of instructions on sorcery or logistics pertaining to human sacrifices. It is a book that reiterates humanistic wisdom—seemingly innocuous. The message can be summarized as caring for oneself above all else (i.e. egoism), in dire contrast with Jesus who expects us to serve others—in families and communities. Although individual rights are fundamental to our North American identity, individualism is not the friend of the Christian. Individual and plastic communion cups popularized during the AIDS scare of the nineteen-eighties send a contorted message to the Christian body, and could only have arisen out of an often shallow Western culture. Harmonious community is tragically reduced to a tray of disposable individuals. Instead, God would have us see ourselves as one indispensable common cup clung between the hands of a single priceless human body composed of various beloved members. God would have us rely on one another in interdependence. Satanism urges its followers to take full control of their lives and depend upon no one but self. Accordingly, fortune telling has never lacked popularity.[20] Horoscopes sell power. People want to know the future so they can change it. We want to be like God. Though much of it is illegitimate and phony, it is undeniable that the soothsaying devil too can perform signs (Rev 16:14). His cunning knowledge of the present enables predictions of the future with an unascertainable degree of accuracy. Ostensibly playful toys can become sadistic snares.

---

20. It must be stated that the Biblical gift of prophecy is not the same as fortune telling. Normally, prophecy is the "authoritative gift of forth telling the messages of God, and not the mediumistic ability of fore-telling the future." Koch 97. In this sense, all faithful pastors are prophets in their preaching. Ultimately, Christian priests unveil God's thoughts about us, in the present, in preparation for our reception of His means of grace. No Biblical prophecy was ever intended to satisfy human curiosity. Every episode involved delivering people the opportunity for salvation.

The Purpose Driven Lie

+ + +

Whether at worship, work or play we are naturally inclined to serve our former master by the service of self. The devil is also obsessed with self-fulfilment in diametrical opposition to the service of others. He adores our ostentatious devotion of our ruthless energy to selfish career objectives or ambitious determinations that assure that our kids turn out more competitive than their peers. Such goals can only be marginally achieved unless driven by wholehearted self-dedication. We love to possess: a title, degree, a larger home. While the devil loves to possess, God prefers to give. From antiquity we have enslaved ourselves to a self-gratifying culture. The difference today is that it is rarely questioned. The ombudsmen have retired their scrutinizing tools. Moral philosophers contribute little to the discourse. Popular celebrities have taken their place. The communists were idealists and romantics. They offered no viable solution to the problems of the sinful nature. However, their social criticism and economic assessment of the Western world still applies. Lenin was right when he accused capitalism of eventually giving birth to its opposite, imperialism, like a monstrous child who consumes its mother.[21] Monopolies and monocultures become inevitable consequences of a free market. Yet we may have no other options. Capitalism uniquely harnesses individual selfishness for the common good. *Accepting* a necessary evil and *loving* it are two very different things. Soldiers are required to kill, but are warned not to enjoy it. The prophet Daniel accepted his position under Nebuchadnezzar. But the working conditions were less than ideal.

Much of the fuel of modern entrepreneurship is selfishness, covetousness and greed, inflaming a society of immediate self-gratification. For example, the slow-paced tempo of a theatre, concert hall, or art gallery has become insufferable to many of the younger generation. "Isn't a synopsis available online?" Survival techniques include interactive museums that entertain and libraries that offer free internet service and DVD rentals. Patience has been crossed off of the list of Christian virtues. Thinking hurts. Christian liturgy is often rejected, even despised, simply because it is misunderstood. An explanation surpassing the duration of a TV commercial is generally not worth listening to. One learns to love the liturgy as one learns to love one's spouse. The consummation of the marriage rightfully follows a patient engagement and familiarization with each other. Love-making only gets easier with time and practice.

---

21. See Lenin, *Imperialism: the Highest Stage of Capitalism*.

Acceptance at the Lord's Table rightfully follows a period of thoughtful preparation. Secular culture demands immediacy. So, sex is anticipated before marriage, customary after a few dates. Holy Communion is demanded at a first visit. We are infatuated by love at first sight. Relying on feelings is easy and convenient. "If it feels right, do it. Who is anyone to judge?" The idea of arranged marriages is horrific to us. Obviously where there are sinners there is abuse, but the assertion that someone else knows what is best for us not only insults the founding principles underlying our liberal democracies but is also received as an intimate slap to the personal pride of independent and self-contained individuals. Yet, do we still believe that *God* knows best? And what about His spokesmen? How counter-cultural are we, really? The proverbial road less-travelled has already been strolled by tens of millions of readers who love bestsellers. The narrow way is a lonely path trodden only by those courageous enough to deny their courage, submit to the notion that someone else knows better, and confess that they too have bought into the devil's lies conforming themselves to the ways of this world (Rom 12:2).

> The Foe in triumph shouted
> When Christ lay in the tomb,
> But, lo, he now is routed,
> His boast is turned to gloom.
> For Christ again is free;
> In glorious victory
> He who is strong to save
> Has triumphed o'er the grave.
>
> Now hell, its prince, the devil,
> Of all their power are shorn;
> Now I am safe from evil,
> And sin I laugh to scorn.
> Grim death with all his might
> Cannot my soul affright;
> He is a powerless form,
> Howe'er he rave and storm.
>
> Now I will cling forever
> To Christ, my Savior true;
> My Lord will leave me never,
> Whate'er He passes through.
> He rends Death's iron chain,
> He breaks through sin and pain,

The Purpose Driven Lie

He shatters hell's dark thrall,
I follow through it all.[22]

---

22. TLH 192.

Le petit prince des ténèbres

> I am sending you to open their eyes, so that they may turn from darkness to light and from the power of Satan to God, that they may receive forgiveness of sins and a place among those who are sanctified by faith in me. (Acts 26:17b-18)

What is it about darkness that makes it so—dark? Why do the Scriptures specify that the disciples brought to Jesus all the sick and those oppressed by demons in the *evening at sundown* (Mark 1:32). "They got into a boat, and started across the sea to Capernaum. It was now dark, and Jesus had not yet come to them" (John 6:17). Why is it that commissioned exorcists pray at 3:00 a.m. during the so called "witching hours"? One individual under demonic influence saw everything as if it was the middle of the night, although it was daytime. This went on for weeks.[1] Darkness typifies the absence of God. When we fall asleep, we experience a microcosm of death. Shortly thereafter we awake and resurrect. Just as the cyclical liturgical calendar mimics the lifetime of Christ, so too the duration of one day represents the span of a lifetime for a Christian.[2] Accordingly, the liturgy is best memorized since it is prayed only once. Each time uttered it happens for both the first and last time. Human beings live exclusively in the present. There is always only one day and one night. For Christians this is pure joy. We have a lot in common with the daughter of Jairus who, though dead, "is not dead but asleep" (Mark 5:39). Whenever we awake, from our beds or from our graves, we find ourselves in the presence of Jesus, which is heaven itself.

---

1. Amorth, *An Exorcist*, 194.

2. Even the seasons of the year remind us of the freezing abyss of death followed by the warm springtime glory of new life and resurrection.

Several evening hymns emphasize this lesson, since one can never be certain as to when or where one will arise. Christian nighttime prayers retain the same goal. Adults plead, "May each day remind us of the coming of the night when no one can work,"[3] while children pray, "Now I lay me down to sleep, I pray the Lord my soul to keep, and if I die before I wake, I pray the Lord my soul to take (and I ask this for Jesus' sake)." Together, we fear the grave as little as our beds.[4] You are not to "let the sun go down on your anger" (Eph 4:26) as we make peace with our neighbours before we die. As the sun sets on the horizon, may the ever more glorious sun of righteousness sink into the darkness of our hearts with a new and radiant light. The *Antiphon* beseeches, "guide us waking, O Lord, and guard us sleeping that awake we may watch with Christ and asleep we may rest in peace."[5] The *Nunc Dimittis* spoken at the end of the *Compline* teaches us that we servants can now rest in peace. St. Simeon was ready to die after witnessing the dedication of the Christ child. With him we too can now happily enter our grave at the close of our day, after hearing the Gospel word. Even more importantly, we sing these words after reception of Holy Communion because we can now die with peace in joy, having seen Christ who had made us His friends (John 15:14–15). Life reaches its pinnacle at the Lord's Table. It doesn't get any better than this. We can now die and rest in the solace of the grace of God "manifested through the appearing of our Saviour Christ Jesus, who abolished death and brought life and immorality to light through the Gospel" (2 Tim 1:10).

+ + +

The devil would love nothing more than watch us deny the way of the true Faith as characterized by the phenomenon of death. Roman Catholic priest Richard John Neuhaus underlines how

> the passion narrative is not simply a playing out of a script that begins with the catechism statement that 'Jesus died for our sins.' His dying is not just a necessary preliminary to the good news of the resurrection. The cross is not just what happened to him—it is who he is. 'We preach Christ crucified,' Paul declares. The God whom we worship is a crucified God. The downplaying of the

---

3. LSB 309.
4. LSB 883.
5. LSB 259.

death of Christ in Christian preaching and piety is a close cousin to the denial of his death. And the denial of his death is a close cousin to the denial of our own death.[6]

However unknowingly, people are assiduously coaxed into inventing a sundry of methods of denying death. We deny His death when we recoil from peering long and hard into our own dark hearts, withdrawing from all of the brutal discoveries. Without an honest assessment of ourselves, we are scandalized by the truth that we worship a crucified man. Like the demons, we shrink away from our creaturely status, and would rather be like God and on our own terms.[7] The cross is foolishness to the neo-Gnostic Christian (1 Cor 1:18) who says, "I already know that Christ died for my sins, so now let's move on. I understand the doctrine of justification perfectly well, so now let us focus on the sanctified life of the new creation, highlighting the fruits of the Spirit, so that I may progress in my faith and righteous living." The allegation suggests that there is something that God neglected to give us at His cross and our Baptism. The unsought-for truth of the matter is that there is nothing missing. The baptismal font and pool of Christ's blood is a refreshing plunge for both novice swimmers and advanced ones since it is, after all, the same pool. Living a righteous life is an honourable goal. It is so requisite that our Lord has already achieved it entirely for us on our behalf. Our striving to become better is a grasping that we are already perfect—in a sense. Thus, we are required to keep on dying.

+ + +

Every theology of glory is expunged before death. One way or another, all eyes are eventually opened to our actual value. At the very least, at the instant of death everything is taken away. No dramatic overture accompanies our ordinary departure from this earth. While giving heed to the words "this very night your soul is required of you" (Luke 12:20) one recalls the Lenten imposition of ashes: "I am dust and to dust I return." One cannot help but repent for one's contribution to and neglect of this broken planet and world. The glaciers are melting, because of me. African children go hungry because of me. I am the sinner, and there is no one else. If the Desert Fathers were correct in instructing that each of us ought to live as if only I and God existed, then I alone am the sinner of all sins, and Jesus

---

6. Neuhaus, *Death on a Friday Afternoon*, 117.
7. Ibid 120.

alone is my saviour. Each of us is responsible for this global brokenness and overarching darkness that dominates all aspects of human existence, which is why Christians pray (for themselves and for all): "Be our light in the darkness, O Lord, and in Your great mercy defend us from all perils and dangers of this night; for the love of Your only Son, Jesus Christ, our Lord."[8] The affirmative response comes at great cost. The Lord of life is so full of life that He must purchase the sins of others in order to die and, thus, burst the bonds of death. The unrivalled Light of the world is so ablaze with unbroken burning light that He must seek out darkness, carrying our sin and strife from within. There is a right way in which a Christian embraces the unholy, welcomes darkness, resists not evil (Matt 5:39) and, yes, is even compelled to sin a little to spite the devil, leaving him no occasion to trouble our consciences by leading us into the fallacy that some "internal light" is the foundation for our salvation and righteousness.[9] At times, we have no choice but to sin boldly, while believing in Christ's merits more surely. The temptation to self-righteousness implodes as we admit that we deserve nothing but death and hell, but have an advocate who stands confidently between Satan's accusations and the magnificent promises that we know to be true.

+ + +

Modern fairy tales have all but entirely erased the disturbing details of Grimm's stories or Aesop's fables, while cute Disneyesque stuffed animals with batteries in their bellies convey more agreeable versions of children's prayers—ones that do not touch upon the morbid subject of death.[10] And yet the lessons somehow do not seem nearly as vital without the threat of real wolves that eat grandmothers or cannibalistic witches who kill chil-

---

8. LSB 257.

9. The following quotation is attributed to Luther even though it is likely derived from the writings of nineteenth-century novelist Elizabeth Rundle Charles: "Whenever the devil harasses you, seek the company of men or drink more, or joke and talk nonsense, or do some other merry thing. Sometimes we must drink more, sport, recreate ourselves, and even sin a little to spite the devil, so that we leave him no place for troubling our consciences with trifles. We are conquered if we try too conscientiously not to sin at all. So when the devil says to you: do not drink, answer him: I will drink, and right freely, just because you tell me not to." Thomas Nelson, *The Chronicles of the Shoenberg Cotta Family*, 1864.

10. The popularized verses include, "Now I lay me down to sleep, I pray the Lord my soul to keep. Guide me through the starry night; wake me when the sun shines bright."

dren. The point was never to traumatize toddlers. It was a didactic method of preparing young hearers for the inevitable tragedies of life, while offering warnings for ever present dangers: "People are cruel"; "You can't trust everyone"; "Listen to your parents."

We Lutherans have often been accused by other Christians as being too negative and pessimistic. Many question our Augustinian emphasis on concupiscence and the deep and profound repercussions of humanity's shared sinful nature. In a debate, the best arguments debunk an opponent's strongest defence, not their weakest. Accordingly, justice assigns defence attorneys even to obviously guilty criminals. Optimism is most optimistic when pessimism is displayed in its most pessimistic form. Expounding the depths of sin's darkness only strengthens the radiance of Christ's grace. Nevertheless, the Eastern Orthodox, preferring to describe salvation in terms of "deification" as a gradual transformation in degrees of holiness, has never appreciated the judicial Pauline emphasis of "penal substitution" or "substitutionary atonement" that informs forensic justification: that although man is "guilty" he is declared "innocent" by the suffering Servant who has chosen to pay the entire debt demanded by the Law. Our righteousness is imputed to us from Christ since we possess no righteousness intrinsic to ourselves about which we can boast.

The theory of evolution originates from a conjecture that the world improves through time. We wish that this were true. It is, however, difficult to reconcile with the fact that we have committed inexcusable crimes against God, our neighbour and creation. Yet the debt owed has been paid. Consequentially, God treats us not as we deserve nor in accordance with our identity as sinners. He treats us as Jesus! The Gospel is the happiest of messages, but refuses to repudiate the reality of humankind's perpetual brokenness. The somewhat mannerist and mildly surreal paintings of Matthias Grünewald which accentuate the severe suffering of Christ have been labelled by some well-meaning Christians as too gory for the Church and counterproductive to a "healthy" view of God's redeemed creation and preservation of His image in man.

Although these accusations may be a far cry from Islam's inability to fathom a holy prophet dying a shameful death (prompting their hypothesis that Jesus was either transported directly into heaven or that He died of natural causes many years later in Kashmir), they do seem to misrepresent the full calamity of the human condition. The fall from Eden was no bruising of the human nature, but a colossal corruption. While some interpret

St. Peter's denial of Christ on that fateful day of trial as an isolated incident, we perceive them as characteristic of our spiritual walk. Only the most scrupulous and honest critical assessments of our spiritual atrocity can lead to lasting hope in the dark moments of despair. When one has an accurate understanding of the gravity of sin, no crucifix will ever be dismissed as "too gory." The bloodiness and ghastliness of the crucifix not only remind us of the terribleness of sin by providing a terrifying glimpse of pure evil, but after the asphyxiation following these realizations they also allow us to breathe easier in the full knowledge that sin can only rest in one place contemporaneously. And if our Lord has absorbed it into Himself, then it follows that it no longer rests upon us. The Reformers popularized this "great exchange": we give Him our failings, hatred, unhappiness, and He offers us His peace, love and joy[11]. What a Christmas gift indeed! If *He* was imprisoned, it means that *we* are now free, and "if the Son sets you free, you are free indeed" (John 8:36). The darker we perceive the prison to have been, the more strikingly illuminating the light. He suffered the immense pangs of hell so that we could escape them all. Besides, if a gory picture of Jesus accentuates the ramification of the serpent's nip on the Lord's heel, how much more gruesome is the wicked one's crushed head (Gen 3:15)? In exhibiting a theology of the cross, the crucifix is the most persuasive image of Christ's glorious victory over our evil nemesis.

+ + +

The military fosters resiliency by preparing for the worst of circumstances. A productive spiritual training is never unmindful of the pervasive presence of evil. Darkness and sin are not phenomena limited to the infamous villains of history, but wedged in the depths of *my* heart and being. Illness can be a blessing in disguise simply because it prepares for the more severe pains and aches that often precede a "natural" death. It acts not only as a reminder of our mortality and inexorable need to trust in God in the present but also diminishes the shock when a painful death occurs. Pain is a kind of "dress rehearsal" for death since we live well when

---

[11] Dr. Martin Luther coined this ancient summary of the Gospel as the *"fröhlicher Wechsel"*: "By this fortunate exchange with us He took upon Himself our sinful person and granted us His innocent and victorious Person. Clothed and dressed in this, we are freed from the curse of the Law, because Christ Himself voluntarily became a curse for us." AE 26: 284.

we die well.[12] Again, sleep is a kind of death; our nightmares a kind of hell. The enigmatic relationship between sleep, death and the demonic became apparent to me as a parish pastor. One demonically oppressed visitor to mass would habitually plunge into sleep at the start of any Christian subject while another undergoing pastoral counselling wished only that he "could sleep forever"—in other words, die. In contrast, Christians are a wakened people (Col 4:2). And though the vigil feels long Christians have hope; just as a slumber is a relief after a long day's toil, so death is our portal to peace and rest. For this reason, believers are rarely spoken of as being "dead" in the Bible but are described as merely "asleep" (1 Thess 4:14).[13] People laugh at Jesus when He says this about the young girl from the house of Jairus. But He is right. The Bible does not intimate that Jesus laughed a lot, but it does say that he was "glad" at the death of Lazarus, so that *we* may believe (John 11:14–15).

+ + +

Much of our discontent with darkness is grounded in trepidation of the unknown. In *The Revelation of St. John* the sea symbolizes unrest and evil, as the ancients had great apprehensions concerning what frightful creatures swam beneath large bodies of waters and the causes of frightening storms. Perhaps the fear of that which lurks within the unsettling shadows is a metaphorical reminder of the deep-seated secret places in our

---

12. Derived from a Good Friday sermon by Rev. Paul Williams in Pembroke, Ontario, 2015.

13. While Christians can boldly and even *joyfully* face death, unbelievers naturally coil away from the subject. For example, the Church continues to witness the decline of attendance at funerals, even though our population is an ageing one. This is not only reflective of the anti-organized religion sentiments in our secularized society, but it also demonstrates a hidden personal terror of the afterlife. Accordingly, funerals are renamed "celebrations of life," and death is mentioned sparsely and often with a friendly smile. Meanwhile the awkwardness of it all is addressed by eulogies consisting of cute and funny stories instead of words that actually heal and help us remember that which is meaningful and lasting. The popularity of conducting such imitative religious services without clergy or in the privacy of one's home is on the rise. This way the family can create their own liturgies or rites themselves, designing the message and aligning the mood in accordance with their own personalized view of how they wish God was and how they believe the universe works. Once again, like the devil, we desire to create our own religion in our own image. Like the evil one, we want to control God and our lives. Yet God continues to give, and freely, while Christianity remains a religion of vulnerability, trusting, receiving; i.e. faith.

own opaque hearts and souls, or the uncomely desires upon which we wish no one to shed light. Darkness hides. Why is it that the interdicted events are often associated with the phenomenon of the night? Drugs. Drinking. Sexual immorality. Is it simply because we attend to our jobs in the day, and that the dark conveniently aligns itself with our "time off" for rest and pleasure, or is there something else intrinsically dark about the dark? Why does the light of the moon and twinkling of the stars spark such joy, even in atheists, while a starless night activates no emotion? Perhaps lights in darkness soothe the simple anxiety of a navigator concerned about the unknown danger of losing his footing or bearings. Or maybe there is something primordial about it all—even spiritual. As evil is the absence of good, darkness is the absence of light. The unholy can only be defined by negative terms. One cannot say what it *is*, but only what it *is not*. Hell is execrated as a hideous place because of its absence of heaven; it is denounced as a dreadful state because of the absence of God. God is forever silent there; His Word no longer spoken nor heard. Hell is dark whereas heaven has "no need of sun or moon to shine on it, for the glory of God gives it light, and its lamp is the Lamb" (Rev 21:23).

None of the artistic masterpieces of Rubens or Dürer do justice in their depictions of the negative afterlife. Because God makes His "sun rise on the evil and on the good" (Matt 5:45) an eternal abode in absolute darkness and emptiness is a torture that finds no parallel in the creation with which we are habituated. For those who love God, hell is absolutely unimaginable since God gives daily bread to evil people too and so the traces of God's goodness infiltrate every aspect of our communal existence. At the same time, His presence is less evident in the dark. Contrariwise, the kingdom of God is a daytime affair. The gloom of the crucifixion happens in the dark from the sixth to ninth hour, while the enlightening resurrection is a morning event. While the world belongs to the anti-Christ—or so it appears—darkness precedes the return of the Christ. Evidently, uneasiness with the dark is natural for those who belong to the light and dwell within this curious spiritual arena in which eternal and temporal realities overlap and intersect: "For you are all children of light, children of the day. We are not of the night or of the darkness. So then let us not sleep, as others do, but let us keep awake and be sober" (1 Thess 5:5–6).

My First Exorcism

+ + +

Some places seem darker than others. Perhaps irrational feelings prompted by memories of disturbing events are easily rectified by some Jungian dream therapy. But still there are places where you somehow know that things are less right than others, even though such an epistemological foundation is unsustainable. We can all recollect times and places that feel, somehow, darker. I myself have experienced this phenomenon as a parish pastor visiting certain homes where something dark lurks. One senses this in countries that seem to lack a Christian population and the influence of the Gospel. Thankfully, God does not withhold His blessings even when they are only for the sake of a few faithful believers. The prayer of one man, Abraham, postponed the falling of judgment upon Sodom. The interceding prayer of our great High Priest alleviates it for eternity. Christians should never underestimate the importance of a prayer, even when it is half-hearted. God is generous. He even loves His enemies and provides for their needs as well, despite their repugnance at, or disbelief in, His presence. Yet still, there are regions where the Word of God is proclaimed less frequently, and true Christians are few. In those places, the lack of God's sacramental presence is noticeable.

Of all the many countries that I have visited, India is one of my favourites. The colourful and chaotic mix of exhilarating atmosphere, enchanting traditions, and stimulating food has few rivals for those who thrive on adventure. Its cultural synergism remains unmatched. Sadly, it is also very dark. When I was sixteen, I had the thrilling opportunity to join a mission team from my church in visiting an orphanage in India that we had funded. It offered us a chance to acquaint ourselves with an institution that we had committed to support financially as well as deepen our Christian ties with their leadership. While there, we also built a church. Like most ecclesiastically endorsed mission trips we likely learned more from them than they did from us. There were six of us in total and I was the youngest. At the end of our stay, we witnessed the conversion to Christianity of several locals in a nearby village where the residents had initially displayed signs of coldness and hostility. After accepting the Gospel, they freely explained their antagonism towards us. Weeks before our arrival, their Hindu priest had warned them that he had had a vision of a visit from six tall white villainous men.[14]

---

14. This is not to suggest that all alleged visions of God are demonic. Some visions lead to Christ. For instance, the influxes of Iranian Christians in the churches of Germany

In a dream, the gods had instructed him to keep clear of these evil intruders and that his people were wise to follow suit. I still recall the red, bloodshot wrathful eyes of this pagan priest—before he became a Christian. After all, the "eye is the lamp of the body" (Luke 11:34).[15]

For those trapped within the constraints of Hindu religion and the heavy burden of its caste system, there is an unfathomable craving for the Gospel. The Hindu gods are a regurgitated version of the Babylonian ones. "There is nothing new under the sun" (Ecc 1:9). All demons seek to enslave. As is implied in Hinduism's offshoot, Buddhism, the human experience is full of such misery that a person's main goal in life is to escape it. Nirvana is a negating happiness, appealing to those who aspire to no longer exist. In no way does it resemble the Judeo-Christian understanding of heaven. New Age Americans may be seduced by the idea of reincarnation with their secret longings to be reborn again as a famous person—for some reason hypnotists and mediums never seem to unearth the past life of their clients as beggars or insects; everyone is always an Abraham Lincoln or Marilyn Monroe. Accordingly, self-righteous North Americans believe that the odds of a better life are in their favour. But reincarnation is not good news. Hinduism believes that reincarnation is the collateral damage of our broken universe. A dampened soul's eventual hope is a dispirited breaking away from the vicious Samsara cycle of rebirth and release into—well—nothingness. *Moksha* is the final liberation from the pitiless cycle and is achieved only after one's debts are balanced out by good Karma. Yet the scales are unwavering. Godliness is the aim. Under the weight of such a belief system grounded upon the ideology of salvation and righteousness earned by arduous good deeds, any unpretentious God-fearer resents birth, embracing the inspirational colloquialism of Taoism: "Better luck next time."

If the gods exist they are not our friends. Neither do they love human beings. To make matters worse, one cannot improve one's miserable station in life. The disenfranchised, wretched, crippled, or those considered "cursed" with the darkest of skin, are considered outcasts, rightly punished for sins accrued in past lives. Their only hope for a more promising future is to live out their horrendous states with dignity and, thereby, earn the necessary Karma for another life. Interfering with one's punishment

---

attribute their conversion to common visions of the Saviour due to their lack of access to the Holy Bible.

15 Although not all displays of red-eye indicate demonic influence, the eye can often confirm the presence of demonic possession when other symptoms of demonic presence are evident.

through attempts at moving from one caste to the next within the divinely construed hierarchy will only ensue in a greater degree of chastisement in the next birth. Fulfilling one's dharma amounts to dutiful acts accomplished between the lanes of one's social level. Christian missionaries were some of the few courageous enough to demonstrate acts of compassion to these "untouchables." The Brahmin priests were stunned when these "white devils" were not struck down by the gods. To the contrary, life in India improved. Cultural relativism shuns interference with cultural norms. North Americans and Europeans judge it all as imperialistic. Access to a zoo of culture suits our consumerist taste buds—the more exotic, the better. It all makes for a more interesting tourist destination. It irks us when these tribal people wear running shoes and listen to radios. It spoils the photo. Their intelligence and our shared commonalities tarnish our fantasy: we want these silly-looking species pure and "untouched" so that they can perform for us and entertain us—like they do for their gods. We radically insist that these atypical cultures are unimpeachably preserved, naively dismissing any questions as to whether or not any elements of these "impeccable" cultural values contradict Natural Law.

Despite reason and intuition, the perpetrators of moral relativism deem all cultural mores as equal. Assertions that female circumcision is exploitative or rape is intrinsically evil imply the existence of objective values and even God. Most postmodern academics and prestigious universities find the price of committal to any truth-claim as holding an absolute value too high. Yet when individuals belonging to the lowest Hindu castes discover that there is only one almighty God, that He is good, taking a personal interest in their lives, offering unconditional love on earth and salvation from their wretched state in the afterlife, forever breaking the vicious and unending "circle of life"—or rather "death"—of reincarnation, and offering to restore them as His children with a one-time permanent rebirth, the immediate attraction of the blessed Gospel is obvious. For them, it is a question of whether or not it is too good to be true. Globalism isn't all bad.

+ + +

During my later travels to Thailand I noticed similar perturbing demonic patterns by those who practice a syncretism between Buddhism, Chinese spirituality and ancestral worship. It was customary for families to give up one of their virgin daughters to prostitution—just for a few years—in order to increase their financial status and their social position. The younger they were, the more lucrative. Such avaricious efforts represented their diabolical solution for advancing to a higher caste, despite risky repercussions in the next life. Forgiveness of sins is purchased in temples enshrining the great Buddha who surrounds himself with gigantic metal cauldrons. The bronze pots are fed by a constant flow of coins clinking and clanking in one harmonious melody of works-righteousness, reminiscent of the perfunctory theological axiom of the Middle Ages, "As soon as a coin in the coffer rings, the soul from purgatory springs," a maxim closely related to, "If you do your very best, Almighty God will do the rest." But what if one's best is not good enough? How many coins suffice? What petrifying surprises wait in ambush for us in the afterlife? Similarly, prayers were purchased and publicized over loudspeakers in hopes that maybe a god or two would be listening in. I wondered if Baal was among the assembly of demons grimacing at yet another incidence of a faith grounded in fear and religion of "Law" fuelled by inventive human attempts at earning salvation and peace with God. The unparalleled religion of the Gospel—that Christ has unilaterally fulfilled all the necessities of the Law and died for those who have not—is our only alternative.

The devil is lord of all belief systems entrenched in the Law. Because he is a thief, each of his innovative worldviews steals away the glory from God as the sole agent in saving dead sinners. Religions of Law seduce individuals into the false belief that they are more morally righteous than they really are, inferring an optimistic ability to cooperate with God in the process of their salvation. The discarding of a monergism of grace results in either Pharisaism or despair. Islam leads to the former. The sinful nature is disparaged—man can please God by his good deeds. There exists an indirect correlation between a high estimation of human moral worth and a deep appreciation for the holiness of God. God's glory is not as glorious when it is easily attained by human efforts. The burka is no blockade to lust. Human imagination is mightier than censorship, since the problem emanates from the darkened depths of a licentious heart. Furthermore, in the Islamic system God is implicitly comprehended as a deity who lacks. His unicity as a singularity suggests that he created mankind out of loneliness. He now commands human worship to improve his low self-esteem. I suppose people love what they know. Even abused children will vehemently defend their pugnacious parent. The God in whom you believe, is the one with whom you are stuck.

Contrariwise, the Triune God is the self-expression of an independent community. He creates out of love, not necessity. As the Cappadocian Fathers remind us, there is only love when there is someone *to* love. Love is relational as it entails an object and a subject. The God who is one is love only because He is three. His love overflows through His creative energies. He creates out of love that floods forth from His very nature. Unlike the Babylonian gods that create slaves to worship them, the true God creates children with whom He chooses to share His life. But what is most striking about Christianity is the belief that God undergoes the whole process of creating us, knowing all the while in His divine omniscience that we would revolt against Him, abuse His love, turn repeatedly away from His fatherly grace, and nail Him to a tree. And yet He so patiently endures it all for us. Although the pains of parenthood are incomparable with the riches of fatherhood or motherhood and children are the cause of unbounded grief strangely surpassed by matchless joy, what kind of love gives birth to, producing life for, a creature that would so mercilessly resent it to the extremity of brutal murder in the first-degree? Only a pure altruistic loves does that. I have often encountered spouses from troubled backgrounds who hesitate in having children because they are afraid of all the risks involved: "would their children turn out okay?" they query. Our God knew the risks entirely, and still chose to have us. In *The Prayer* Leo Tolstoy tells a story about the loss of a mother's cherished child to a dreadful disease. While the disillusioned mother clutches his cold, stiff body in grief she complains to God about the injustice of it all: how her innocent tiny infant had never hurt anybody—*yet*. For her lament is interrupted by a vision depicting what her angelic son *would* have eventually become: an exploitative rapacious drunkard.[16] God had hindered this agonizing future-possibility, saving her. She regrets her prayer and only wishes that she could dispel the painful image of her deviant adult son. But the living God isn't like that. He gives birth to us anyways. Economists speculate that the legalization of abortion in the nineteen-eighties has reduced the crime rate twenty years later in the American inner-cities because potential criminals from the lower class never had the chance to breed. Yet our God is not a pragmatist—He considers all life as precious, even when we do not. Each person is, singularly, the apple of His eye (Ps 17:8). The irony is that God offers the only innocent life—the only worthy life—to redeem all the rest. "A life for a life," after all. What conceited man may mock as masochistic, our Lord describes as love.

---

16. Tolstoy, *Divine and Human*, 39–45.

Le petit prince des ténèbres

+ + +

Just as perceptions of love amongst people vary, so, too, religions are not all the same. The devil knows this well. Faithful Hindus undertake pilgrimages to wash themselves in what is considered to be the sacred river of the Ganges. Ironically, it is one of the most polluted places in the world. Sewage is not the main concern. The ashes of the dead are spread out over the stagnant waters. Because the poorest cannot afford an adequate measure of wood to burn corpses, they often only partially succeed.[17] The semi-burnt bodies are deposited into the river with the ashes. Compounded by unbridled sewage run-off, this allegedly "holy" stream becomes a poisonous and hazardous swimming pool while millions of pilgrims annually wash therein and sip from the disease-ridden sludge. Surely the devil laughs as people fall mortally ill. Each god demands its special means of worship. Rotten fruit litter the base of statues of Shiva, while the Dalits go hungry. Idols "have mouths, but do not speak; eyes, but do not see... Those who make them become like them" (Ps 115:5, 8). The multiplicities of gods worshipped are all counterfeit deities. They are demons because God alone is One: "What pagans sacrifice they offer to demons and not to God" (1 Cor 10:20). The dark kingdom's intrinsic hierarchical structure and the demons' competitive drive prove a lack of complete omnipotence on the part of any single one. Their display of many of the same sinful qualities found among humankind only betrays the true identity of each and every one of these "gods."

+ + +

Hinduism raises the question as to whether or not demons are territorial. Does it make any difference that the god Vishnu rules one city while the god Ganesh functions as the patron saint of another? Many sensationalist "Christian" fiction novels on spiritual warfare inevitably feed off of this theme of demonic territorialism. Perhaps there are some hidden truths imbedded in the story lines. The Christian Orthodox preserve a ritual of

---

17. Crematoriums do not publicize their logistical challenges. For instance, it is next to impossible to totally burn a cadaver. The remainders of bones are usually ground down to the smallest pieces possible. Sometimes miniscule fragments get mixed into other urns. No furnace outside of hell is hot enough to do the trick. The mourning Indians have even greater tactical concerns with regards to their burial rites.

exorcism intended to combat evil spirits in a community or locality.[18] Many Protestants, in an effort to avoid superstition, slip into the opposite error of hyper-reasoning. However unintentional, conjecturing our own responses to questions that the Holy One has chosen not to answer infringe upon God's sovereignty. By definition, mysteries are unexplainable. This bugs us. The Greek word *mysterion* is translated into Latin as *sacramentum*. North American Christians are perplexed and even irritated by the sacraments. With the exception of detective novels that always provide tidy solutions, people in the Western world do not, generally, like mysteries. We expect answers. We insist upon transparency. Magicians are cute, but they annoy us too: "There must be a plausible explanation and why don't I have it?" No-one likes to be left out of a secret. Liberal democracies handle the concept of exclusive and privileged information as personal insult. We believe that we all have an intrinsic *right* to know—*everything*. The principle of equality necessitates it. The devil was right. It would be nice to be like God. It's only fair.

The reformer John Calvin best represents the quest for theological explanations in his pursuit of a gapless continuity regarding all matters pertaining to the kingdom of God. As a brilliant lawyer, his dogmatic systematics strove to answer all spiritual questions. Every theological matter had to hang together like the component parts of a tight operational machine. From a "reasonable" human perspective, his sacraments make sense. They minimize unanswered questions. In contrast, Eastern Orthodox theology today evades the issue of systematizing dogma with the preamble that all Christianity is mystery, concretized through the practice of a personalized mystical spirituality aimed at the deification of the individual believer. Their theological dialogues do not resemble the Western methodology. Instead, they occur in conversation between liturgy, patristic writings and iconography. On the one hand, there are certainly enviable aspects to the Orthodox expression of the Christian Faith such as an admirably deep reverence for the unknown and hidden counsels of God, a careful handling of the mysteries as genuinely sacred, and a holy fear in the looming presence of the awe-full mystery—all of which are esteemable. On the other hand, the contention that all questions of faith are enveloped by unfathomable mystery is easily governed by a relativistic epistemology paralleling that of popular existential spirituality today: no one is allowed to judge another

---

18. *The Ancient Orthodox Ritual of Exorcism*, 24.

person's relationship with God as they encounter Him through the Church's religious mediums.

The new religious climate has redefined the parameters of pastoral concern, counsel and discipline, which have become increasingly ambiguous. Moreover, how can anyone appraise allegations of workings of the Holy Spirit, whether it is through dreams, visions, or heart-felt insights, if rigid Christological principles of doctrine are, for all practical purposes, deemed inapplicable? For the Orthodox, the Holy Spirit proceeds from the Father and not the Son, in contrast with the *filioque* of the Western version of the Nicene Creed (i.e. that the Holy Spirit proceeds from both the Father and the Son). Fortunately not a solid wall, but still a semi-transparent hedge is wedged between the Second and Third Persons of the Holy Trinity. The Augustinian shape of the Holy Trinity in the Western Church reinforces a common and united vision between the Holy Spirit and the Son. In short, the Holy Spirit serves the mission of the Son. He creates faith in the Crucified Lord, who is the Way to the heavenly Father. Are the Orthodox teachings of the Orthodox Church still entirely orthodox? The Orthodox believe so. Yet the vicissitudes of their pneumatology are not as impregnable a shield as they may believe. But then again, I am applying tools and corollaries of my Western dogmatic assumptions to my evaluation, which is culturally insensitive and politically incorrect—or so I am told.

Yet the weaknesses of the Orthodox Church today do not diminish the redeemable qualities pertaining to their reverent worldview and profound belief in holy phenomenon and spiritual realities hidden inside of physicality. Ritual enactments cannot simply be reduced to symbolic gestures—they are spiritual war. While serving as a pastor in Montreal, I frequently observed Greek Orthodox believers crossing themselves whenever they walked by a church building in respectful appreciation for the presence of the consecrated host on the other side of the walls—often locked in, what is appropriately called, a "tabernacle." It was their way of saluting the invisible yet ever-present Saviour who continues to dwell with the faithful. Little do they realize the pointlessness of the earnest gesture when the majority of churches in North America do not believe in the corporal presence of Christ in, with and under the consecrated elements. Many churches remain empty of the true body and blood of the Lord. But in other churches, out of respect for God's presence, believers are instructed to genuflect as they enter a silent sanctuary. Silence is a normal reaction to awe. Because most Protestants have become inclined to thinking upon Jesus as their Facebook friend, they forget that He remains almighty God. They ungracefully manage worship space as they would their common living room. Pious believers opting to pray quietly in the pew instead of socializing with neighbors are often perceived as rude. The vessels that just moments before contained the life of God—the creating energies of the universe—are treated as common dishes, or even thrown into the trash.[19]

In spite of these popular trends, there are still many exceptions to such clumsy abuse—thanks be to God. Some still insist on celebrating funerals at their undexterously-designed churches with steep stairs and narrow narthexes, and burying their dead in the tiny adjacent cemeteries, even though funeral parlors are more convenient. Yet cremation remains the preference. We live in contradiction. Most churches, even those that customarily project a "casual" view of God, still ceremonially deconsecrate the sanctuaries when the building is sold to a condominium company. Theologically, the underlying attitudes that drive these paradoxical practices are difficult to reconcile. Customs surface from competing worldviews, and do not simply demonstrate different applications of the Holy Scripture or commentaries of the Church Fathers. They manifest doctrinal beliefs in the daily practical application of a life of prayer. The Church does not mandate genuflection or a respectful attitude towards a church building. Yet to neglect such common piety is somehow unholy. Demons disrespect the things of God. They are known to speak out of turn (Mark 1:25). The indwelling Holy Spirit seeks no association with these enemies. By the *external* reading of the words of Scriptures He chases them away. Although Western Christians residing in a desacralized society have a tendency to *internalize* God's Word by reading it "in our heads," children are encouraged to pray the Apostles' Creed and the Lord's Prayer *out loud* while suffering a nightmare (and with a special emphasis on the words, "deliver us from the evil one"). If children are the optimal model of faith (Luke 18:17), we adults have a lot to learn from their example.

Because of the omnipresence of Christ by His glorified human nature, all physical things become spiritual, however vaguely. At the same time, there are certain spaces that are somehow, noticeably, *sacred*. It is just not clear how. Sometimes the laying on of hands and the touch of water helps to exorcize demons. Sacraments propose junctures between the realm of

---

19. Conversely, often Satanists and occult practitioners go to incredible lengths in acquiring a consecrated host or drop of sacred wine for their unholy rituals. Who would have thought that the devil was such a master teacher of theology, namely, the real presence of Christ in the Eucharist?

heaven and that of the earth. For a thousand years Roman Catholics have conducted pilgrimages during Holy Week to the sites of Martyrs at the Vatican. There is nothing received there that cannot be received elsewhere, and yet, there is something sacred about the space and time. Aboriginal disputes over burial sites cannot flippantly be reduced to greedy grabs for capital property. Even the Old Testament saints such as Jacob insisted upon being buried with the Fathers. Furthermore, it is a cop-out to argue that space *becomes* sacred solely based upon the significance it may carry for the worshiper. The corporal cloth marks the actual borders between consecrated elements and regular bread. St. Paul's handkerchief was employed for exorcism and the healing of diseases (Acts 19:11–12). But even if the Shroud of Turin proved illegitimate and pilgrims no longer expected healing from it, they wouldn't use it as a bathrobe either. God has touched certain physical things and places, and so, by respecting them, we offer homage to Him.

Believing that we are surrounded by the sacred governs our behaviour for the better. Some have entertained angels unaware (Heb 13:2) while others, demons. Likewise, although we do not worship our ancestors, we are surrounded by a "cloud" of them (Heb 12:1). The saints are the friends of God. I do not invoke them, but God forbid I speak poorly about them. Those who do talk to saints or angels are sometimes falsely accused of idolatry. Along with offering their petitions directly to God through Jesus, all Christians ask terrestrial saints to pray for them, while others also ask the celestial ones to join in. Praying to someone is not necessarily the same as trusting in them. And I appreciate that they pray for me since I can use as much help as I can get.

Some exorcists contend that the intercessions of the saints, angels, and the Holy Virgin have proven very effective in their ministry. Godly practices and customs handed on to us from our forefathers and foremothers are to be treasured by God's children. They originate from our elders who were not only wiser than we are, but lived in closer temporal proximity to the Christ event than ourselves (2 Thess 2:15; 1 Cor 11:2). In other words, despite self-evident business principles replicated in the latest fashionable Christian leadership paraphernalia, followers of Christ do not gaze into the future. Rather, they stare back into the past because of the bearing it has on the present. Because the future does not, and has never, existed, it is "of all things, the thing least like eternity"[20] while "the present is the point at which

---

20. Lewis, *The Screwtape Letters*, 48.

time touches eternity."[21] Epistemologically, we read the book of the present, using the language of the classics. Hermeneutically, we evaluate the events of the present through the lenses of the traditions of the Church, gifted to us by the Holy Spirit through the sacrament of Holy Baptism. We hear the opinions of *the now* through the voices of *the then*. Thus, fortunetellers are handmaidens of the devil. So are end-time preachers since Jesus said that we are not to obsess with knowing the hour for His return (Matt 24:36). Sometimes old is better than new. Despite public opinion, the elderly are, in general, smarter than the younger. The Church Fathers are wiser than us as well. We would not pray "Thy kingdom come" and "Come Lord Jesus" unless we were a tad fatalistic. Our Advent hope and yearning for Judgment Day remains anchored in the conviction that the future is bleaker, even if simply because we are further away from Christ, not in space, but through time as we advance through history. It is our way of respecting the gamut of time as created by the Creator.

+ + +

Returning to the question of demonic territorialism, one wonders whether or not the demonic retinue "Legion" was restricted to the region of the Gerasenes? It really makes no difference to me as a Christian. As an ambassador of Christ I am assured that "There is no fear in love, but perfect love casts out fear" (1 John 4:18a). Roosevelt's acclaimed quotation, "We have nothing to fear but fear itself" is insightful. With the king at your side, there is never reason to fear a rebellious prince, no matter how maleficent he may be. Christ descended into hell to proclaim victory and set its captives free. Although it may not jive with our spatial and ontological understanding of the afterlife (weren't the Old Testaments saints *already* present in heaven?) the point is that the joyful Easter message of Christ's death and resurrection has crushed the power of the devil, sin and all of evil's hold upon humankind with finality. Fear is what inhibits us from taking flight through the unlocked prison gate. Lacking faith induces us to remain huddled within hell's agonizing yet familiar clutches. Besides that, the descent into hell demonstrates that there is no terrain foreign to the Messiah. He underwent the "walkthrough" through hell, which surpasses the vastness of planet earth's core and is more dreadful than the pictorial depictions of a Hieronymus Bosch. Jesus has paraded His presence up and

---

21. Ibid 49.

Le petit prince des ténèbres

down the streets of hades in a victory march. All the armies of hell remain subdued as God the Almighty occupies their homeland. There is no escape from His presence "who is over all and through all and in all" (Eph 4:6). "If I ascend to heaven, you are there! If I make my bed in *Sheol*, you are there" (Ps 139:8). Therefore,

> I am sure that neither death nor life, nor angels nor rulers, nor things present nor things to come, nor powers, nor height nor depth, nor anything else in all creation, will be able to separate us from the love of God in Christ Jesus our Lord (Rom 8:38–39).

The military centurion in the eighth chapter of St. Matthew's Gospel is sage to apply his understanding of authority from the temporal realm to the operative principles of the spiritual one (Matt 8:8–9). If he, being a mere man, is able to order compliance simply by his verbal injunctions, how much more obedient are all the powers of the universe to the commanding words of their omnipotent Creator as spoken through the mouth of Christ Jesus the Lord? We are wise to imitate his faith as he seeks one thing from Christ: a word from His mouth promising hope in light of the human experience of darkness. God's mouthpieces are nearby. If only we believed.

+ + +

Is the awareness of sacred space by large numbers of believers indicative of a "Christian" society? Let us not fool ourselves by relying on observations, intuitions, feelings and sentiments that suggest that the unreached zones on earth are penetrated by a vastly greater degree of demonic activity than our modern, civilized and "Christianized" societies. The so-called Holy Roman Empire may protest, but the concept of a Christian society is a myth. All Christians live as pilgrims within a society. Albeit when they are a majority, an undeniable Christian "flavour" is injected into the common culture with welcome effects. Christian morality still shapes the behaviours of Western people today. Even atheists appeal to the Golden Rule and Christian understandings of justice. But for how long will this continue? Their parents have passed on to them these crumbs of true religion. But like Hansel and Gretel we are running low on bread. Certainly, democratic ideas derived from the doctrine of the universal priesthood and the importance of the individual as reflectors of the image of God remain imbedded in our civil laws. But laws are amended by humans whenever they are judged to be outdated. The revamping of the sexual education curriculum

My First Exorcism

in our public schools to include guidelines pertaining to oral and anal sex is an easy target. Etiquette continues as an extension of the common morality of a culture. Yet morality must at the very least be founded on a notion of a higher power as the "ground of all being."[22]

No one disputes that our culture is becoming increasingly, and truly, secular. But without God, to whom are any of us accountable? One advantage of the Islamic State is that citizens continue to share a common etiquette aligned with a discernible moral compass—necessary "glue" for a healthy society. Etiquette develops over time. Without an ethos underlying the ways we live and the manner in which we think and reason, we regress. Etiquette distinguishes us from other creatures, like beasts, or even demons. We may be technologically advanced and flaunt ourselves as more secure and safe than those "religious" societies before us. Naturally as we stand on the shoulders of prior generations, we may indeed appear as giants. But this apparent stability is attributed to the lessons that we have inherited from others through time and is not necessarily an indicator of our own advancement. The Egyptian pyramids of Giza surprise us because *we* would have been unable to achieve *their* ingenious feats given their technological constraints—and even, sometimes, our own! Evolution is the epitome of arrogance. We think we are better than them. Maybe Satan is right: the attainment of divine status isn't as far off as we once thought—we just need to generate enough "positive energy."

We believe that the present is always superior to the past. And yet unlike many ancient and "backward" civilizations we remain fragmented. We lack manners and a common ethos while our classical moral philosophers lay embalmed in the crypt of a history textbook. Islam is patient. Shi'ite extremists are cognizant of the signs of a severely crippled and unhealthy society. Etiquette does not express optional and convenient norms intended to assure more orderly society. It offers a safety net of protection against ourselves; agreed upon principles defining what we understand to be good, true and noble. Without detectable directives, we play a game without any rules. We maintain government, but may still be on the edge of anarchy. The romantic revolutions of the eighteenth-century were unpredictable and unforeseen. Yet they did not lack unity, leadership or precision. The inventors of democracy presupposed like-minded individuals, presuming them to be not only well-informed and educated, but also adherents to the same moral view. The lowest common denominator with which we all agree

---

22. A phrase attributed to Paul Tillich.

is plummeting with little notice. Although patience is a godly attribute, the devil also appears to possess it to some degree. And he too loves diversity. Where God brings unity, the devil seeks division. The opposite holds true as well. Our splintered society will instigate consequences that not even the most arrogant apocalyptic preacher would dare to announce. Yet, as is true of all waves of fierce persecution, the end-times' afflictions will only bind us together closer. And though authentic Christians will remain and the true Christian Church will persist, we should prepare ourselves for some unlikely allies (Mark 9:39–40). The Church has always resembled a motley crew—an odd looking body, but the glorious body of Christ, nonetheless.

> What harm can sin and death then do?
> The true God now abides with you.
> Let hell and Satan rage and chafe,
> Christ is your Brother—ye are safe.
>
> Not one He will or can forsake
> Who Him his confidence doth make.
> Let all his wiles the Tempter try,
> You may his utmost powers defy.[23]

---

23. TLH 103.

Why I am not *not* a Christian

> Therefore, rejoice, O heavens and you who dwell in them! But woe to you, O earth and sea, for the devil has come down to you in great wrath, because he knows that his time is short! (Rev 12:12)

If demons exist, it would be foolish for the business of the day to continue as per usual. Unbelievers can be likened to the citizens in the disease-ridden village in Albert Camus' *La Peste*, most of who simply choose to ignore the existence or urgency of the fatal epidemic that surrounds them. Lethargic creatures we are.

There are certain key decisions that we make in life that affect our eternal landing place; decisive intersections along a path directing us towards a limited number of destinations. A Christian couple's decision to cohabitate outside of God's holy institution of marriage leads them on a catastrophic migration down a dark pathway as they eventually sever their ties with their church. The counterfeit happiness achieved parallels a paradise lost in eternity. A seemingly harmless postponement of marriage through even a short lived period of fornication, distances the unrepentant couple from the source of their love, setting them upon an unstable tide away from the blessed solid ground of their spiritual homeland. Meanwhile, to our astonishment, a Christian ex-occultist consciously decides to re-invite the devil back into his soul, once swept clean by the workings of the Holy Spirit. The latter may strike us as more horrific, but both are equally dangerous. However, by the grace of God, despite the permanent temporal damage in either case—such as an augmentation of diabolical activity or an unplanned pregnancy—there is still hope and redemption. The forgiveness of God traverses the widest oceans. Even the most frightening alleys in hell have not been left untrodden by the ubiquitous presence of our almighty and merciful king.

+ + +

I believe that I have engaged in battles with the devil through demonically oppressed and possessed individuals. But the most nefarious manifestations of evil are not encountered in demoniacs. Rather, we meet them every day in the cultures from which we are bred, the messages to which we are exposed, and even the ideas and passions to which we are committed. The devil, a compelling impersonator, masquerades as an angel of light in the manners in which we perceive our surroundings, creeping into the filters with which we screen information and interpret our experiences. Demonic activity, in other words, is not usually obvious. My first exorcism gave me a glimpse of the face of evil. But there are uglier images habitually hidden behind a mask of good intentions, cultural norms or personal preferences. Though inconspicuous, the veil hides an even more hideous make-up.

Admittedly, these reflections are based more or less on personal experience. Truth ought never to be founded on one's subjective life experience, since how one sees and feels about a thing may be totally disconnected from reality. I may experience a bad dream, not because I am under demonic ambush, but simply because I ate spicy pizza and Buffalo wings the night before. God's Word is the sole foundation for truth and not our lifelong experiences or impressions, no matter how intriguing we may be to ourselves. We have a solemn warning in Jacob's wrestling with the divine man in the book of Genesis: even God may resemble the devil at times.[1] The desert is metaphorical of the deathly, dry and destitute periods of our lives. The Bible often records demonic activity occurring in the desert. Perhaps God is accustomed to this strategy in ensuring that we do not stray from the narrow way. Going undercover achieved Him victory at Calvary. St. Ambrosiaster preached a clever sermon comparing Eve's temptation

---

1. We find that God often hides His glory behind various dark masks in order to teach us to walk by faith. Our eyes are unreliable, our emotions fluctuate and the meaning or relevance of our personal experiences is open to all kinds of metaphysical interpretations. But when we place our footing upon the solid rock of God's solid and unchanging Word, we no longer stand on sinking ground: "When darkness veils His lovely face, I rest on His unchanging grace; In every high and stormy gale, My anchor holds within the veil." LSB 576.

to bite into the fruit with the devil's determination to bite into the Christ, consuming Him at that first service of *Tenebrae*. Yet he is quelled by the same method that he had employed; foiled by his own trap. The very means of victory is the ironic method of His defeat; victory hidden in loss. Glory cloaked in tragedy. Just as the dark prince conceals himself in light, so too the Lord of Light is disguised in darkness, draped beneath shrouds with which we are all too familiar. The Messiah handed Himself over to His unsuspecting enemies in silence. He offers Himself willingly to the Hellish hordes. And for a brief moment, they are permitted to do whatever they please, subjecting Him to hideous abuses. As the Father turns His face, Jesus absorbs the iniquity of the world into Himself like a vacuum drawing all the filth of humanity into His very person. He is transformed into sin for us. He *had* been forsaken by God. It was the only way that the darkness could be overcome with finality; the superlative destruction of all that separates unholy creation from a holy God. The temple curtain dividing mortal man from immortal God is torn forever.

The greatest miracle is not that Jesus dies, but that He allows Himself to be "possessed" by evil entities, to do what they wish with Him for a moment—a *very long* moment—that resulted in our mind-boggling release from their clutches. The unmitigated agony that this "Man of Sorrows" (Isa 53:3) must have felt, forsaken to a darkness in complete contradistinction with His divine nature and unity in the Godhead, is entirely incomprehensible to us sinners. Forest fighters fend off fire with fire. They employ the tactic of backfire in order to contain a spreading fire—setting a controlled wood ablaze to halt the extension of the flames to new parts. Thousands of trees and square footage of wildlife space are sacrificed. "For our sake he made him to be sin who knew no sin, so that in him we might become the righteousness of God" (2 Cor 5:21). The Lamb of God is set ablaze on the altar of a tree. Butchered and sent among the wolves, for us He died. Origen believed that if there is a hell, it must be empty. Every Christian should pray for that (1 Tim 2:4). Even though it is no longer as easy to get to hell—Jesus Christ has singlehandedly accomplished all that is necessary for our salvation by His atoning death—heaven holds no prisoners. God takes no hostages. The Holy Spirit forces none to enjoy His gifts. Residents of hell are volunteers.

The vocabulary of hell is vast and the demons are fluent in every language both modern and archaic, but victory is a term with which the devil is entirely unfamiliar. Because of Christ, he only knows defeat. The devil possesses none of the inhabitants of hell. He has not hijacked hell but is rather its most pitied prisoner. All of its occupants are independent, each from one another and entirely from God. There is no team, no gang, no community—just a bunch of individuals subsisting side-by-side, together-alone. The punch line to this comical tragedy is that the inhabitant's life-long prayer has been answered in the affirmative: "Please God, leave me alone." This unrepentant company of angels and people have finally gained separation from their Creator.

Nevertheless, all synonyms for hell are incapable of relating the torment felt by the evil one, whose zeal failed to achieve complete autonomy from his Maker. Even "under the earth," the demons will be forced to proclaim that Jesus Christ is Lord (Phil 2:10) and will never escape the searing memory of their holy and loving Creator. For, despite his most ambitious efforts, the devil will never cease to remain un-god. He has nothing; Christ has all. His hands are empty; our Lord's are full. Hell is dark. So is earth. But it is a darkness that Christ Jesus continues to overcome (John 1:5). Concealed behind all dark clouds is the bright-shining Son of God with His impenetrable radiance and inextinguishable grace.

I don't believe all things happen for a reason. Christians should favour Biblical promises over anachronistic signs and other omens in decision-making. Christians who make fleeces seek to control God. There is no divine plan that has orchestrated the clumsy spilling of my coffee on my lap. The "reason" is my own stupidity. Except with regards to matters of salvation and Christian conversion, we live with the choices that we make, and, thankfully, God walks with us in spite of many of them. But some things do happen for a reason. The seeming meaninglessness of an innocent man beaten and crucified to death is the most critical one. The *reason* is the salvation of all humankind. "It is finished" are the most momentous words ever spoken. Through them, His destiny was determined and our fate was finally seized and sealed—by faith.

In the meantime, may the supplication of the *Compline* echo the weary rhythmic hum of our soul's incessant yet hopeful plea: "O Lord, support us all the day long of this troubled life, until the shadows lengthen and the evening comes and the busy world is hushed, the fever of life is over, and our work is done. Then, Lord, in Your mercy grant us a safe lodging and a holy rest and peace at the last; through Jesus Christ our Lord. Amen."[2]

---

2. LSB 257.

The Bridegroom soon will call us:
Thus God shall from all evil
Forever make us free,
From sin and from the devil,
From all adversity,
From sickness, pain, and sadness,
From troubles, cares, and fears,
And grant us heavenly gladness
And wipe away our tears.[3]

---

3. TLH 67.

Epilogue
The Death of a Sales Pitch

> There shall not be found among you anyone who burns his son or his daughter as an offering, anyone who practices divination or tells fortunes or interprets omens, or a sorcerer or a charmer or a medium or a necromancer or one who inquires of the dead, for whoever does these things is an abomination to the Lord. And because of these abominations the Lord your God is driving them out before you. (Deut 18:10–12)

The world of spirits is different from the world of men. The Sadducees speculated about the physics of marriage in heaven (Matt 22:23–33) and we too wonder about the dynamics of spiritual activity on earth. Can spirits of the deceased be summoned from the dead, as was the case with Samuel (1 Sam 28:7–20)? Reputable sources report on the spirits of the damned in hell entering the body of a demoniac alongside their demons. Even Judas has allegedly been heard. He apparently has a reputation for tempting the despairing towards suicide. If the spirits of believers are the saints who join the heavenly choirs in worship, perhaps the same holds true in the theatrics of the underworld. "Birds of a feather flock together," or as our Lord observes, "Wherever the corpse is, there the vultures will gather" (Matt 24:28). Ultimately, we know very little and that is probably best. No two exorcisms are the same. Like people, demons have their own personalities and names. Likewise they are not all deterred by the same means. Some find it excruciatingly painful to be touched by a stole since the stole and the laying on of hands not only symbolizes, but demonstrates, the power of the priesthood. Accordingly, Christian Orthodox exorcists sew stoles together "in order to have a very long stole to extend from the priest to the victim's neck."[1] Other demons detest the sound of chanting, the smell of incense, the sensation of an exorcist's breath on its face, physical gestures and images of the holy cross, and the use of holy water.[2] Celebrating mass in a "haunted" house has also proven to be very successful. Although the remedies may vary, and like any physical illness the treatment may last a lifetime, one thing is clear: it is the Word and power of Christ that compels. And when we acknowledge the demons disguised in ordinary life—masked in the subtleties of our thoughts, words and deeds—we discover that the weapon remains unchanged. Although all prayers and blessings improve the situation, unsuccessful exorcism can be mostly attributed to the unwillingness of the possessed to be completely delivered. We all have our choices. Our Lord does not take prisoners.

In both the case of individuals and a society, we discover an indirect correlation between faith and demonic activity: where faith decreases, the influence of the devil increases. In an increasingly neo-Gnostic culture, on a timeline that inches ever closer to the Day of our Lord, we can expect more visible manifestations of evil even in our so-called "advanced society." The medical world is already overrun by the demands placed upon it by the mentally and emotionally disturbed. As a Church, we too have choices. Although church attendance plummets, desire for our services and curiosity regarding our message is escalating to new heights. Here the Emerging Church should be envied for their proactivity and commitment. But do the rest of us have the Christian desire and courage to engage in that conversation with today's "tax collectors and sinners"? Withholding pearls before swine can become an all too convenient out.

Perhaps faithful churches will face a day when strangers knock on their doors, not with funeral or wedding enquiries, but with requests for exorcisms, house blessings and spiritual deliverance. But first people need to be convinced that there is no such thing as a "friendly ghost." But "how are they to hear without someone preaching?" (Rom 10:14b) The job is ours and we ought never underestimate how well we do it—just ask the converts who are forever grateful. Although our supposedly dying churches are tempted to sell (or, dare I say, "prostitute") themselves to religious consumers as they compete with the rhetoric of "contemporary" and "relevant" and other seductive criteria that have little to do with the Gospel, deep down in obstinate hearts hover lost souls hungering for true Christianity.

1. *The Ancient Orthodox Ritual of Exorcism*, 1.
2. Ibid.

Epilogue

People who are lost in darkness thirst for prayers, seek for blessings and some yearn for exorcism. In light of this dangerous and appalling cultural milieu a portentous question remains for the Church: do we turn inward upon ourselves—as is the way of the demons and is the natural inclination of every sinful creature—or do we reach outwards towards the other in need, as is the way of the Christian?

I thank you, my heavenly Father, through Jesus Christ, Your dear Son, that You have graciously kept me this day; and I pray that You would forgive me all my sins where I have done wrong, and graciously keep me this night. For into Your hands I commend myself, my body and soul, and all things. Let Your holy angel be with me, that the evil foe may have no power over me. Amen.

—Martin Luther's Evening Prayer

Bibliography

Adams, T. *The Christian Treasury containing contributions from ministers and members of various evangelical denominations*. London: Groombridge and Sons, 1881.
Amorth, Gabriele. *An Exorcist Tells his story*. San Francisco: Ignatius, 1999.
Amorth, Gabriele. *An Exorcist: More stories*. San Francisco, Ignatius, 2002.
Ashcraft, Jack. *The Ancient Orthodox Ritual of Exorcism* (ed. Fr. Jack Ashcraft). J.L Ashcraft, 2011.
Augustine of Hippo. *The City of God* (trans. Marcus Dods). New York: Random House, 1950.
Bennett, Robert H. *I Am Not Afraid*. Saint Louis: CPH, 2014.
Bonhoeffer, Dietrich. *Life Together*. New York: Harper and Row, 1954.
Bonhoeffer. *Meditations on the Cross*. Louisville: Westminster John Knox, 1996.
The Catechetical Lectures of St. Cyril, Archbishop of Jerusalem (trans. Henry Newman). Whitefish: Kessinger Publishers, 2007.
Chrysostom, John. *Old Testament Homilies* (vol.3). Brookline: Holy Cross Orthodox, 2003.
Exorcism: The findings of a Commission convened by the Bishop of Exeter (ed. Dom Robert Petitpierre). London: W. Hart & Son, 1972.
Foucault, Michel. *Discipline and Punish: The Birth of the Prison*. New York: Vintage Books, 1977.
Foucault, Michel. *Madness and Civilization: A History of Insanity in the Age of Reason*. New York: Vintage Books, 1965.
Gerhard, Johann. *Meditations on Divine Mercy*. Saint Louis: Concordia, 2003.
Giertz, Bo. *The Hammer of God*. Minneapolis: Augsburg Fortress, 1960.
Guazzo, Francesco Maria. *Compendium Maleficarum*. New York: Dover Publications, 1988.
Hallesby, Ole. *Prayer*. Minneapolis: Augsburg Fortress, 1994.
Jabès, Edmond. *From the Desert to the Book: Dialogues with Marcel Cohen* (trans. Pierre Joris). New York: Station Hill, 1990.
Kleinig, John W. *Grace upon Grace: Spirituality for Today*. Saint Louis: CPH, 2008.
Koch, Kurt E. *Occult Bondage and Deliverance*. Grand Rapids: Kregel, 1970.
Koenig, Harold G. *Faith and Mental Health*. Philadelphia: Templeton Foundation, 2005.
Lenin, V.I. *Imperialism, the Highest Stage of Capitalism*. Peking: Foreign Language, 1975.
Lewis, C.S. *The Screwtape Letters*. New York: Time Incorporated, 1961.
Lewis, C.S. "The Humanitarian Theory of Punishment." In *First and Second Things*. Glasgow: William Collins Sons, 1985, p.96–114.

Bibliography

Lewis, C.S. *The Lion, the Witch and the Wardrobe*. Harmondsworth: Penguin, 1950.

Löhe, Johann Konrad Wilhelm. *Seed Grains of Prayer: a Manuel for evangelical Christians*. Chicago: Wartburg, 1912.

Neuhaus, Richard John. *Death On a Friday Afternoon: meditations on the last words of Jesus from the cross*. New York: Basic Books, 2000.

Nouwen, Henri. *The Return of the Prodigal Son*. New York: Doubleday, 1992.

Petersen, David H. *Thy Kingdom Come: Lent and Easter Sermons by David H. Petersen*. Fort Wayne: Emmanuel, 2012.

Pieper, Francis. *Christian Dogmatics vol. III*. St. Louis: CPH, 1953.

Postman, Neil. *Amusing ourselves to death*. New York: Penguin books, 1985.

Riddle, John M. *Eve's Herbs: A History of Contraception and Abortion in the West*. Cambridge: Harvard University, 1997.

Ristau, Harold. *Understanding Martin Luther's Demonological Rhetoric in His Treatise Against the Heavenly Prophets (1525): How What Luther Speaks Is Essential to What Luther Says*. Lewiston: Edwin Mellen, 2010.

Rites and Resources for Pastoral Care. Lutheran Church of Australia. Adelaide: Openbook, 1998.

The Roman Ritual (trans. Philip T. Weller). New York: Bruce Publishing Co., 1964.

The Service Book and Hymnal. Philadelphia: Lutheran Church in America, 1958.

Smith, Preserved. *The Life and Letters of Martin Luther*. Boston: Houghton Mifflin Co., 1911.

Taylor, Charles. *Sources of the Self*. Cambridge: Harvard University, 1989.

Tolstoy, Leo. *Divine and Human and other stories by Leo Tolstoy*. Grand Rapids: Zondervan, 2000.

Townsend, Tim. *Mission at Nuremberg*. New York: HarperCollins, 2014.

Treasury of Daily Prayer. St. Louis: CPH, 2008.

Vogl, Carl. *Begone Satan! A soul-stirring account of Diabolical possession*. Rockford: Tan books and Publishers, 1973.

Walsh, Froma. *Strengthening Family Resilience*. New York: The Guilford, 2006.

Walther, C.F.W. *Walther's Pastorale: American Lutheran Pastoral Theology* (trans. John M. Drickamer). New Haven: Lutheran News, 1995.

Walther, C.F.W. *God Grant It*. Saint Louis: Concordia, 2006.

Waltzer, Michael. *Spheres of Justice: A Defense of Pluralism and Equality*. New York: Basic Books, 1984.

www.ingramcontent.com/pod-product-compliance
Lightning Source LLC
Chambersburg PA
CBHW051932160426
43198CB00012B/2126